Praise for Barbara Annis

Thank you Barbara for the most enlightening two days of Executive Coaching. I have seen so much light shed upon a potentially frustrating topic called Gender Equality. I will use it in every way I can.

General Ernest Beno, U.S. Department of National Defense

This was the first time in two years as Deputy Minister that we really had an open and honest conversation. I found this a powerful watershed experience. Thank you!

Morris Rosenberg, Deputy Minister, U.S. Justice Department

As a practitioner toiling diligently in the arena of gender awareness, executive coaching, and personal transformation, Barbara Annis is a living legend. She has been a locomotive for change in the corporate world for over 20 years. In that time, she's pulled desired changes out of over 50,000 business executives and professionals in over 2,000 workshop seminars. . . . She unleashes the energies we need to envision and deliver futures we've only vaguely dreamed. And she does it by empowering teams of men and women to work in transformative partnerships, in collaborations that turn gender differences from a liability to an engine of new abilities.

O. Woodward Buckner, Chief Executive Officer, Buckner & Co.

Same Words, Different Language makes sense of the neurological differences between the genders. It builds a new form of conversation between men and women. More importantly, it builds a new form of collaboration. For over 2.5 million years, men and women have worked together to accomplish unreasonable outcomes during unreasonable times. But they've barely begun to tap the powers of their synergy. *Same Words, Different Language* is a seminal contribution to this new level of inquiry.

Howard Bloom, author, The Global P̶̶̶̶̶

There is a new frontier awaitir̶ ̶ ̶ r in Annis' adventures on the oft̶ y,

relationship, and gender awareness management. *Same Words, Different Language* is the outcome of 3,600,000,000 man/women hours of live transformational interactive experiences. I suspect cultural anthropologists, semanticists, neuroscientists, psycho-social biologists, strategists, organizational behaviorists and talk-show hosts will be 'plumbing the gold' from this practitioner's treasure mine of real-world experiences for many years to come.

Chief Comentator, Business News-CNBC;
Former Chairman of the FDIC & RTC

Barbara, thank you so much for mastering this crucial topic; it has created so many breakthroughs in my life as a boss, a husband and a father.
Executive, Honeywell

Barbara has an ability to engage people in such a brilliant manner, that we (both men and women) are left with the feeling of being empowered and validated.
Colonel, U.S. Army

I used to be just angry at men, saying 'they don't get it!' I now realize that I too didn't 'get it' about them. Now I can really see and appreciate the differences.
Diane, Xerox Executive

Teaches you 'life skills' that are valuable far beyond what we do at the bank.
Vice President, Personal Banking, Bancorp

I can honestly not find anything less than outstanding in this course. Excellent facilitation.
Vice President, Chase Manhattan

Thank you, thank you. I always thought that men were the ones who needed to understand; little did I know that I had a lot to learn about my own misinterpretations. I am so relieved that I can actually be a women at work instead of a man in women's clothes.
Cathy Diamond, IBM Executive

The honesty and openness of communication with resolution was fantastic.
Vice President, Marketing, IBM

Excellent program; best 48 hours spent on a course, a real eye opener.
Senior Vice President, Investment Banking, Wood Gundy

Excellent program – every executive should experience this. Provided true value throughout the entire session. I benefited both personally and professionally.
Senior Vice President, General Motors

I didn't know what to expect, and being a man, I was very careful on the first day. What a positive surprise! I actually enjoyed every single minute, while learning more that I have in any course. This was a watershed moment for all of us.
Deputy Minister, U.S. Treasury Department

Thank you very much! I really enjoyed this. This was the best course I have ever taken, and as a lifelong learner that says a lot.
Jim Beqaj, Senior Vice President, Nesbitt Burns

All I have to say is: where was this 20 years ago? It could have solved so many business and personal issues for me, and perhaps even saved a (my) marriage.
Partner, Deloitte & Touche

No one better than Barbara Annis can show you how to build a high-performing culture of inclusion. Years of extensive research and practical experience have given Barbara a unique perspective on how to overcome the deeply entrenched obstacles that create invisible chasms in organizations. Her incisive views on how men and women can most effectively work together will guide you in developing a leadership context where all differences can become complementary strengths.
Hubert Saint-Onge, Chief Executive Officer, author, Levering Communities of Practice for Strategic Advance

same words
words

different
language

same words

different language

Why men and women
don't understand each other
and what to do about it

Barbara Annis

PIATKUS

Copyright © 2003 Barbara Annis

First published in 2003 by
Judy Piatkus (Publishers) Limited
5 Windmill Street
London W1T 2JA
e-mail: info@piatkus.co.uk

The moral right of the author has been asserted

A catalogue record for this book is available from the British Library

ISBN 0 7499 2351 2

Edited by Krystyna Mayer and Nigel Copeland

This book has been printed on paper manufactured with respect for the environment using wood from managed sustainable resources

Typeset by Palimpsest Book Production Limited, Polmont, Stirlingshire
Printed and bound in Great Britain by
Butler & Tanner Ltd, Frome and London

Contents

Dedication

I dedicate this book to everyone committed to making a lasting difference in their relationships.

To my wonderful children, Lauren, Sasha, Stéphane and Christian.

To my life-time partner, Paul, whose indubitable love and integrity I always admire and treasure.

Acknowledgements

I thank Julie Barlow, who co-wrote this book with me, for all her hard work. I wish to thank the many thousands of men and women who have participated in this work and have ensured that it made a lasting difference in their lives. I also want to acknowledge my friends, colleagues, and clients for having made tremendous contributions in their sphere of influence: Shahla Aly, Donna Marie Antoniadis, Sharon Bartlett, General Ernest Beno, Chantal Bernier, Josee Bouchard, Linda Bowles, Woody Buckner, Barbara Burns, Charlie Coffey, Tony Comper, David Creelman, Paul Currie, Judy Dahm, Leslie Danis, Susan Delacourt, Bill Etherington, Michael Hagerman, the late Dr. Willis Harman, John Hunkin, Dr. Susan Hutton, Benedikte Jacobs, Dr. Saj-nicole Joni, Kevin Keliher, Pat Kennedy, General Kinsman, Anna Kirk, Mary Ellen Koroscil, Uno Langmann, Rob Largen, Maria LeRose, Dr. Dawna Markova, Debbie McGrath, Marguerite McLeod, Stephanie McKendrick, Ken Nason, Jill Nyren, Morris Rosenberg, Cynthia Rudge, Hubert Saint-Onge, Vicky Saunders, Victoria Slager, Dr. Janet Smith, Gina Sparrow, Carol Stephenson, Susan Tanner, Jim Ward, Dr. Sandra Witelson and Sabrina Yamamoto.

Introduction

Whether you are a man or a woman, I'm sure you'll recognize the woman in this story. Men sometimes call her 'The Dragon Lady' or 'Iron Lady'. Women may call her a 'man in women's clothes'. It's a challenge to work with her.

That woman was me. The time was the early 1980s. The place was the multi-national firm Sony. I was climbing the corporate ladder, well on my way to becoming Sony's first female sales manager. It had been a tough journey, but I made it to the top and raised three children at the same time. I felt that I had scored a great victory for women. I was sure my story would inspire working women everywhere.

And I was sure I knew the formula for success: you had to behave like a man. Life at Sony was hectic, tough and competitive. To tackle all the obstacles in my way, I attended – literally – 100 coaching sessions on topics ranging from assertiveness training to 'guerrilla war tactics for women'. The sessions were more like military training camps than anything, but I kept going to them. Why? They worked. I won more outstanding performance awards than any of my colleagues did. I became such a tough manager that some of my colleagues nicknamed me the

Sherman Tank – most male colleagues indirectly called me 'tough broad'.

Like many working women at the time, I believed that to be equal to men women had to be the same as men. Actually, back in the 1970s and 1980s, many feminists believed women had to be the same but *better* – women had to study more, work harder and perform better than men did to succeed. Basically, everyone thought the only model for success was the male model. No one thought much about gender difference back then. Like every one else, I thought that being different meant being inferior to men, or less than men. I bought into that thinking. I was a split personality: a man in the office, and a woman in my personal relationships and with my clients.

I actually bought into the 'same is equal' thinking so much that I decided to help other women learn to act more like men too. After all, it was the way to success.

When I looked around, I saw a lot of women struggling to make it in the corporate world, but not that many actually running companies or sitting in boardrooms. I was sure it was because women weren't trying hard enough. I believed women were self-defeating and took things too personally, or just failed to make themselves heard. I told women to get off it and stop being drama queens. That's what the men said – and I bought into it. I told women they had to become powerful, authoritative and assertive, and that they had to suppress their emotions and talk like a boss. It worked for me.

I stuck to this crusade for several years until one fateful incident at a workshop I was giving for women at the pharmaceutical company SmithKline Beecham. When I look back now, I can see how that workshop turned my whole world-view upside-down and led me to do the work I do today.

The workshop had started in the usual way, with me preaching on about how women had to take control of their lives. When I got to the part about gaining respect from your boss, one woman in the group stopped me.

'Why are you saying it's women who have to change?' she asked. 'What about men?'

In my mind, different meant less. There was a hierarchy, and women were lower on the ladder. I told the woman, 'If you're here, it's because you're missing something.'

She didn't buy it. 'We're not here because we think something's wrong with us. The problem is in the work environment. It is devaluing. That's all.'

I stuck to my line. 'If you feel devalued maybe there's something wrong with the way you put yourself across.'

But the woman didn't buy that either, and neither did any of her colleagues at the workshop. Exasperated, I ended the workshop and sent them home.

I also went home – to think. And that's when I began to see that I had been getting it all wrong, all along. I understood that there was no point trying to make women act like men. Women were different from men! At the time, I was also giving workshops to men on how to relate to women. The men actually acted very differently in workshops than the women did. They didn't nod while I was speaking, like the women. They didn't collaborate or brainstorm in the way women did. They didn't draw up lists in the same way or discuss things in the same way either. When I thought about my work at Sony, I realized that men and women worked differently there, too. I had always chalked these differences up to personality, but I started wondering if there wasn't more to it than that.

Well, that was when I decided to see what scientists and researchers were saying about gender differences – and they had a lot to say. By the mid-1980s, the facts were there. Men and women really were different. They think differently. They process information differently. They communicate differently. What a huge mistake it had been to try to turn women into men.

Seeing the Difference

Ever since that fateful workshop at the pharmaceutical company, my life has been dedicated to showing men and women how they are different, and helping them overcome the challenges caused by their differences. In the last 20 years, my associates and I have listened to over 50,000 men and women across the planet talk about the challenges they experience working with the opposite sex. I have listened to managers, doctors and nurses, lawyers, accountants and bankers, soldiers and secretaries, stockbrokers, scientists, politicians and more – practically all the job descriptions you can imagine. I have also worked with more companies in Europe and North America than you can imagine, including IBM, Xerox, General Motors, The Body Shop, Honeywell, Deloitte & Touche, and many large insurance firms, banks and government agencies.

Over and over again, in real-life work situations, I have seen how men and women think and communicate differently. And I have seen how these differences cause misunderstandings that provoke more misunderstandings, and leave everyone angry and frustrated.

Whether you are a man or a woman, you are bound to recognize and identify with many of the individuals and scenarios on these pages: people who feel undervalued or excluded at work, companies who can't hold on to talented employees, people who think there is nothing they can do to improve their working environment, people who 'leave and stay'.

As you read these pages, you will see what's going on. You'll see inside the mind of the other sex. You'll see how your own gender-related behaviour contributes to misunderstandings with it, and how gender differences create situations where talented workers feel alienated but don't know why. Why does this happen? Because men and women see different realities, hear different stories, assimilate information differently and communicate differently. We use the same words, but we speak different languages.

In this book, you'll learn to overcome the misunderstandings caused by gender difference. You'll learn how to put yourself in the shoes of the other sex, how to really listen to it, how to avoid common misunderstandings and how to get your own message across.

I did not write this book to prove that men and women are different. The idea that men and women are different, and that these differences create misunderstandings, has been around forever. In the early 1990s, John Gray published his famous book *Men are from Mars, Women are from Venus*. In 1991 linguist Deborah Tannen also wrote her groundbreaking book *You Just Don't Understand*, on how men and women communicate differently. My goal is to take you one step further.

I want to give you the 'eyes to see' gender difference so you will learn how to overcome the misunderstandings and challenges differences create. In these pages, you'll see what the latest scientific research says about how men and women differ. You'll hear the voices of real men and women talk about the challenges of working together. And you will learn how to make the most out of your own strengths and those of the other sex.

You may have picked up this book for a variety of reasons. Maybe you've heard about gender differences already. Maybe you suspect that some of the problems in your work environment are caused by gender difference, and you want to find solutions. Maybe you're a company leader trying to figure out why the employee turnover rate at your company is so high. Or maybe you are just unhappy at work. No matter which category you fall into, I guarantee this book will help you improve your working relations with the opposite sex. You will gain insights and tools and learn how to:

- Recognize how your words and actions impact on others.

- Fine-tune your listening so you really hear what the other sex is saying.

- Make convincing arguments to the other sex, in terms they understand.

- Sell more effectively to women (women represent 80 per cent of consumer spending).

- Coach and mentor the other sex more effectively.

- Get better result from mixed teams, and have more fun working together.

- Earn the trust and respect of your co-workers and improve your relationships.

- And enjoy your job more!

But first, a few words of caution. *Same Words Different Language* is not a 'women's book'. Gender differences create challenges for everyone. It is not strictly for work, either. This book is for everyone who wants to understand the other sex and enjoy working with them, whether you are writing an annual report, or raising a family. Most of the case scenarios I talk about come from the working world, but the lessons of this book go beyond the workplace. We all relate to both genders in some shape or form, every day of our lives.

At the end of the trip you'll take through these pages, you'll see that while men and women are different there's a lot more uniting them than dividing them. People basically want the same things from their work: the feeling that they are contributing and that they have the opportunity as individuals to learn and grow.

As you journey through this book, you may discover that you have more prejudices and pre-existing ideas than you think. Be ready to face your prejudices, and face them honestly. You will only have the 'eyes to see' when you understand yourself. Getting those eyes is a bumpy trip, but it will change your life. You'll see.

Barbara Annis, August 2002

CHAPTER 1

It's the Environment!

Water to the fish, air to the bird, both can't see it, but they can feel the turbulent forces of change.

Stephen Covey, author, *Seven Habits of Highly Effective People*

The first time I talked to them, they told me they were the kind of law firm that young lawyers were 'dying' to work for. But from what other people had told me about them, I suspected people were dying *from* working there. I was right. In the last year, seven of their top lawyers, all women, had left. The women said they left for 'family reasons' or 'work-life balance'. I knew there was more to it than that.

It really was an impressive law firm. It had huge, luxurious offices and a client list packed with FTSE 100 companies. Working there was every young lawyer's dream. The partners at the firm wanted the best talent at any price. Naturally, they had no problem attracting the cream of the law school graduates. Yet something was going wrong. Several of their top female lawyers had left recently, as well as other talented younger male and female lawyers, but predominantly females. They didn't see a trend, but one of their clients did. The client, a bank I worked for, gave the law firm my number. 'You people need help,' they said.

When I started meeting senior partners and employees at the firm, I saw the problems right away. Both men and women at the firm complained about the working environment. One younger partner told me that the senior partners regularly made derogatory comments about women. Several people mentioned the seven women lawyers who had left the previous year. 'Oh yeah, there was that long-legged girl who was working for us,' recalled one of the senior partners, conjuring up what seemed to be an already indistinct memory of one of those women; he thought she'd left for family reasons. A junior partner told me about a dinner party where senior partners exchanged sexist jokes while the women at the table stared stonily, pretending not to hear or rolling their eyes in the best good humour they could muster up. That gave me a good idea of the kinds of problems they were probably having.

I decided to meet up with the long-legged girl, whose name was Sandra. As it turned out, she hadn't left her job for 'family reasons' at all. Shortly after she left, she launched her own firm. A single mother with a ten-year-old daughter, Sandra welcomed me into her stylish new office. Trained in a top law school, she had all the polish and assurance to show for it. Her new firm was doing lots of business, and professionally, she told me, she was a lot happier now.

Slowly, the story of why she had left her old job unfolded. Sandra had suspected it would be a tough place to work for when she was hired. It was, but she stuck it out for 12 years. 'I had genuine commitment to the firm and to the work I was doing,' she told me. 'But then it just got to be too much. I couldn't stand the atmosphere any more. At the end, I had to drag myself to work,' she said. What was going on?

As Sandra put it, no matter how hard she worked and no matter how many hours she put in, she never felt that she was regarded as 'one of the boys'. At meetings, the partners would discuss business as if she wasn't even there, she said. 'I didn't feel valued,' Sandra said. 'It got to the point where I had to admit that nothing was improving.'

It was a shame, she said, because she loved working with her clients and found the atmosphere stimulating. That's what kept her going for so long, she said. She had thrived on the challenging client relationships, carefully honing her skills as a lawyer. But at some point it occurred to her that she worked in two worlds. Her clients treated her like a professional and her associates continually treated her as though she were a subordinate. Sandra felt as if no one valued her or recognized her unique skills, and she felt she wasn't being given the responsibilities she deserved. So she decided to move on. As she put it, 'What choice did I have?'

To avoid having to explain, she told her associates that she needed more time with her daughter. They were surprised, and sad to see her go, but they took her at her word. Everyone left it at that.

The Women's Story

I knew it wasn't that simple, and I knew it wasn't just Sandra's story. I arranged to meet up with six other women who had left the firm the previous year and see what they had to say. Their complaints were exactly the same as Sandra's. They said they weren't treated like equal colleagues no matter how much they worked. They felt they were constantly singled out as women and never considered on an equal footing with their male colleagues. They felt they were viewed as being 'less confident' but weren't sure why. Every time they asked a rigorous question it was turned back onto them, as if their colleagues thought they were being suspicious rather than simply seeking information.

One woman complained to her associates that she was never given high-profile cases. 'Women work on these cases but we are never in the limelight.' The women felt they were being paid even less respect than their junior male colleagues were. They said the support staff gave a lot more 'support' to men than to them. I asked the women how their male colleagues reacted when they tried to talk about these issues. 'They told us we were exaggerating, or that we were over-personalizing. They said we were being overly critical or making a mountain out of a molehill.'

In the end, these women, too, felt overworked and under-challenged and not valued by their colleagues. They were paid less and felt they got less respect than their male colleagues. All of them said that one of the worst feelings they had working at this firm was that of isolation. They weren't part of the boy's network, but there was no girl's network. They felt as if they were on their own, adrift in problems that couldn't be broached with anyone else, let alone be solved.

So like Sandra, they talked with their feet. And since the women were sure no one would understand their real reasons for leaving, they each gave the easiest, most legitimate excuse they could think of, a variation on the same theme. Several called it 'work-life balance', a catch-phrase for 'family'. The rest said they needed more 'flexibility', a word which, to their lawyer partners, sounded like about the same thing.

The partners believed the women's excuses. Everyone took the women's words at face value. 'Leaving for family reasons' had a familiar ring to it. As some of the partners told me themselves, 'It goes with being a woman.' It was predictable. None of them made the connection between the atmosphere they described to me and the women's departures. Seven senior lawyers out of the door in one year, all women, and no one saw a trend!

How the Penny Dropped

But there *was* a connection. My colleague Andrew and I had interviewed almost everyone working for the firm, either individually or in focus groups. Many employees felt the firm's environment was dominated by patronizing behaviour. Of course a lot of women felt this way, but surprisingly, so did a lot of men. Many of the lawyers complained about a macho atmosphere, elitism on the part of senior partners and a 'star status' attributed to certain partners. They resented the turf wars, and the endless meetings, which certain partners attended but others weren't invited to. Many men confessed that they were uncomfortable with the environment at the firm, but that they were afraid to bring up their concerns with the senior partners. There was a lot of pressure on them to conform.

Needless to say, the partners were not too happy to hear these complaints when I told them about the results of my interviews. True to their lawyer's training, they particularized or picked apart every complaint set before them. They demanded examples of patronizing behaviour, then dismissed those examples for one reason or another. They said things like, 'Oh, it must have been so-and-so that said that. She has it in for me.' I reported that one woman said that she was tired of being patted on the head and of being told not to worry her little head over things. The woman was, in fact, petite. 'I know who that is,' blurted out one partner. 'She just has a short-person complex. That's got nothing to do with gender.'

Their response to the complaints: kill the messenger. If I had left them to it, they would have spent the entire day dissecting each issue to satisfy themselves that none of them held water. There were moments when I wished I could just leave them to their own bickering, but I pressed on, trying to steer through the acrimony until the senior partners saw what was going on.

Suddenly, after several hours of arguing, the tone in the room changed. One of the women in the group had decided to speak up. She was their top litigation lawyer. Up until then, she had been silent. She looked at the senior partners and said, 'You regard me as if I were your daughter. You may not realize it, but that's what you do.' She told them how humiliating she found their behaviour.

Suddenly, the lights started going on. It was like opening the floodgates. 'You mean, I do that?' one man uttered. When the partners started to see how their own actions impacted on the women working at their firm, all the themes we had been discussing took on a new light. Until then, no one had actually made a connection between the departure of the seven women the previous year and the complaints others were making about the environment. The partners all saw them as 'isolated' incidents. Then, all of a sudden, everyone saw the women's departures as part of a big problem: the working atmosphere at the firm was corrosive. The atmosphere wasn't actually killing individual people, but it was quickly killing the firm.

It didn't take the partners long to see how much the bad atmosphere was costing them. Everyone knew that when the women left, they took valuable clients with them. Everyone was aware that losing those clients had cost the firm millions in lost business. When they calculated the total cost of seven lawyers leaving, it really sunk in.

'I reckon we have a problem,' one partner concluded.

'I think that's putting it mildly,' said another.

It may be tempting – and satisfying – to see this as a tale of twenty angry lawyers learning a lesson about how they paid a high price for treating women badly. The male partners at the firm said and did things that were offensive to women. The women eventually threw in the towel and took business worth millions with them. Andrew and myself made the men aware of how they had caused the women's departure, and they resolved to change their ways. There's even a happy ending.

Well, maybe Hollywood would like it, but in reality, this story has just begun. Solving the problem in this firm, as in most companies, is not about finding a villain, and deciding who's right and who's wrong. It's not about men 'learning their lessons'. It's about changing an environment that's hurting everyone. Law firms, banks and large international accountancy firms aren't the only places where corrosive work environments make people feel alienated and frustrated. I see those environments in all kinds of organizations and fields: sales, manufacturing, retail, public service, engineering, universities, architecture.

The good news? Each of us can help change that environment, no matter where we work.

The situation in the law firm, like that in every company or organization I work for, is the result of misunderstandings. Those misunderstandings start because men and women differ in fundamental ways: in how we think, how we communicate, how we assimilate information, and more. When we don't understand those differences, we project our reactions on to the other sex and judge them, without ever understanding the real message or what their behaviour really means. Both men and women play an equal role in the misunderstandings.

And both men and women can change their behaviour. It all starts with identifying the environment in which we spend so much of our working lives, and in doing what we can to make it a place we enjoy working in, and where we can all thrive.

The Fish Aquarium

If you only get one lesson out of this book, it's this: men and women are two different kinds of fish. You're probably wondering: so what's that got to do with anything? It explains a lot more than you think!

I compare today's work environment to an aquarium where beautiful red fish have been flourishing for years. One day, you decide to add blue fish. If it worked for the red ones, it'll work for the blue ones, you tell yourself. They're both fish, after all. The only difference is their colour. But when you add the blue fish, something goes wrong. They don't like it. They don't flourish. The water doesn't seem to suit them, and pretty soon they start to make the red fish unhappy, too. The conclusion is inescapable. If you want both fish to flourish, you have to change the water.

That's where the workplace is right now. There's something wrong with the water we're swimming in. No one is happy in the fish tank. Most women aren't happy at work. And neither are most men. It's not women's fault. And it's not men's fault. It's the water we're swimming in.

Most companies that come to me for help think they have a 'women's problem'. Either they've had harassment charges brought against them, or they're losing women and don't understand why. Sometimes companies call me because an inner group – usually women – has got together and decided something needs to be done about how women are treated there.

While most of the business leaders I meet know that there is a problem in today's workplace that needs to be addressed, many believe it's just a matter of 'getting the numbers right'. A manager from the Department of Works and Pensions in London recently told me: 'Just look at the facts. The policies are there to ensure equality between women and men.' But a young investment banker attending one of my workshops in the UK said: 'Our bank is proud of the progress we have made with our female staff – that out of thirty-six women, we even have two at the executive management level.' Other companies I see boast about how their programmes to promote women in management or through their special women's networks are 'taking care of things'. But nothing could be further from the truth.

The truth is, women feel the water we're swimming in more than men. It's no mystery why. Despite the fact that women make up the majority of both university undergraduates and the top college graduates in business, law, accountancy, medicine, sociology and education, and despite their massive entry into most areas of employment, and their having climbed to the top tiers of management everywhere, the working world remains for the most part designed according to a male vision. That's not men's fault!

Women weren't around when the model was developed in the last century. Over the centuries, men have written the basic rules for how almost everything in the office gets done: from writing reports, to conducting evaluations to how board meetings are run. Those rules have stuck, even though they don't reflect the way many individual men would now choose to run things.

Traditional and New Business Models

The traditional business model is so common and so universal that no one even notices it. It's invisible, like water is to the fish. Yet it was essentially written from a mindset that makes sense to men: it's a sports model, based on a military model of command and control. It looks roughly like this:

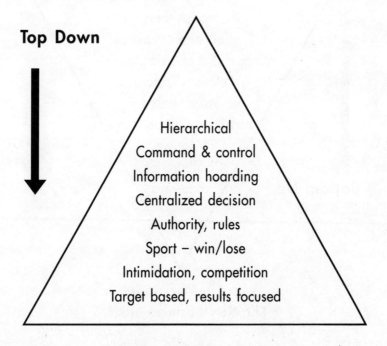

The Traditional Business Model

Why do women struggle with this model? It simply doesn't correspond to the way they naturally think and work. If women were left to their own devices, they would write a very different set of rules for the business world. Women naturally seek collaboration and cooperation. Women have a completely different view of what 'team' means, how teams should function and what their objective is. Women almost always try to advance projects by achieving consensus. Does this sound like an unfounded generalization based on traditional ideas about women? Lots of people might think so. But it's true. And not only is it true – it constitutes one of women's greatest strengths in business. In fact, women's 'natural' model looks a lot like the new 'bottom-up' style that many of today's businesses are trying to adopt.

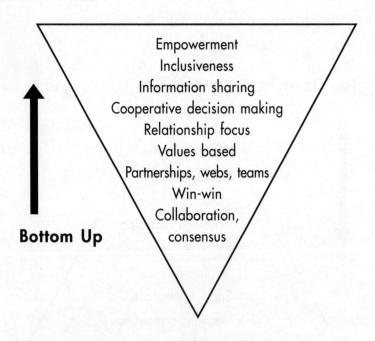

Bottom Up

Empowerment
Inclusiveness
Information sharing
Cooperative decision making
Relationship focus
Values based
Partnerships, webs, teams
Win-win
Collaboration,
consensus

The New Business Model

The Traditional Model for business is a fish tank women don't thrive in. When men work within a different 'model' in a female-dominated structure, they too feel like they're in foreign territory!

Nathan, a young male manager and the only man on the team of the famous international skin products company, The Body Shop, headed by Anita Roddick, told me he was unfamiliar with his company's way of making decisions. The Body Shop functioned on the female bottom-up, collaborative model. While the Traditional Model focuses on a goal and finding the means to achieve the goal, the Body Shop model focuses on empowerment, building trust between co-workers and collaboration. This model was completely counter-intuitive to Nathan. 'I can't believe we ever get anything done.' The New Model works well at The Body Shop – it has the sales to prove it – although it was foreign territory to Nathan. He was just used to working with the Traditional Model.

For women, the traditional working environment feels like a kind of silent, ongoing culture shock. That's probably why almost half the women I meet in workshops are considering leaving their jobs. 'The workplace just isn't conducive to women,' they constantly tell me.

Women's culture shock starts after university, the last time when men and women work in genuine team spirit before heading out into the real world. In the workplace, men naturally shift to the hierarchical mode. It's as if they're running on an old team games model. Men's teams have 'leaders', 'stars' and a distinct structure from the outset. The teams only exist to meet targets, to 'win'. Terms like 'partnership' and 'team-building' have become very stylish in the business world these days but in reality, men's idea of teamwork still follows the same old model. A good team player is someone who follows the boss.

For women, the environment in most offices makes them feel as if they are in a foreign country without a guidebook. That creates frustration, and sooner or later, women's frustration rubs off on men.

Everyone's Problem

That's where today's workplace is. Everywhere, large numbers of people are unhappy at work. To some degree, a recent international study by Gallup offers a good illustration of how low worker morale really is. The study questioned 1.7 million workers in 101 companies in 63 different countries. The workers were asked whether they 'felt they had the opportunity to do their best every day' at their job. Only 20 per cent of employees said yes. Only one-fifth of today's workers feel they are getting the opportunity to put their personal strengths and talents to work. The study found that the longer the employees stayed in their jobs and the higher they climbed the traditional career ladder, the less they felt they were giving their best stuff at work.[1] When 80 per cent of employees feel they aren't making the contribution they could be making at their jobs, there's clearly a problem.

You're probably thinking, 'Okay, there's a problem. But it's only in traditional businesses or old-fashioned companies.' That's a modern myth. Everywhere I see men and women working together, they are encountering the same problems. Even modern high-tech companies aren't exempt from the rule.

No one is happy. The common wisdom is that working women want to spend more time with their families. But the reality is that everyone does, men and women alike. What most of the women I meet really want from their work – and what they're not getting – is the feeling they are doing something meaningful and that they are valued. Most men I meet feel this way too.

The problem in today's workplace is not a 'women's problem'. Companies, organizations and associations of all types need to learn how to make use of both men's and women's strengths. That's the only way to change the water in the fish tank so everyone will be happy.

Only a very few, maybe 5 per cent of the companies I meet, understand that the issue in today's workplace is not 'treating women better' but changing the environment of their company so women will feel comfortable, so they'll flourish.

Mike, senior manager at the accounting firm Deloitte & Touche, is one of many men who have told me how concerned they are about getting and keeping women employees. 'I know there's something about the environment that alienates women,' he told me. 'It's not discrimination, really. It's just subtle differences in the way women are treated.'

Mike is among the more enlightened business leaders with respect to gender awareness. These precious few already understand that gender communication problems are a business problem. They know the growth in their company – their fish tank – will be held back unless they find a way to change the water.

The Solution? Change the Water

So where do we start? The first step in overcoming gender-based misunderstanding is to realize that men and women are really two different kinds of fish. That's a surprisingly tough concept to get across these days. Over time, feminism has taught us that 'equal' means 'the same'. It doesn't. Men and women don't think the same way. They don't communicate the same way. They don't hear the same things when they are spoken to and they don't mean the same things when they speak. Of course we understand each other – enough to live and work together. But a lot of the time, we just think we understand when we don't. Miscommunication feeds misinterpretation. Feelings get hurt without anyone understanding what has happened, and when that happens, nobody wins.

It's always tempting for women to say: 'Men have to change. That will solve all our problems.' But that way of thinking won't get you ahead, neither men nor women. It's a mistake to think that if women are losing out, men are winning. It's not a zero-sum game. Gender-based miscommunications hurt everyone. The environment is not men's fault, and the way to fix it is not as simple as getting men to change. As much as men need to understand how women think and communicate, women need to understand men's style, their need for goals, targets, structure and hierarchy, among other things. Women need to learn to place men's actions in this context; not to just 'accept' men for what they are, but to understand where they're coming from.

Men need to do the same thing in regard to women. They need to hear where women are coming from, and they need to be able to walk a mile in women's shoes. The only way they can do this is by understanding how women are different. Women think differently. They assimilate information differently. And they communicate differently.

This book is about changing the water in the fish tank. It's about turning a no-win situation into a win-win situation. The idea is not to throw out the old model once and for all and replace it with the new model. There are situations in business where the old model still works well, where hierarchical, centralized decision-making is pretty effective. But the *environment* has to change. The water that the old model creates has to go. No one is happy working in that water any more. So how do we change it? By developing congruence between the old model and the new model, recognizing the special strengths men and women both bring, and knowing how and when to put those strengths to use. When you do that, the water in your office will change. Not only will women be happier working in that water, everyone will. You'll create a work environment that:

- Encourages open and honest communication.

- Fosters the continual development of all employees.

- Recognizes and appreciates everyone's achievements.

- Creates pride and joy in the organization.

- Mines the gold in people.

- Builds trust and values.

- Liberates rather than controls.

- Engages in participatory management.

- Inspires through visionary leadership.

- Applies an inclusive not an exclusive approach to gender difference.

- Respects the individual and values integrity.

- Promotes individuals' strengths rather than criticizing their weaknesses.

The secret to changing the water is understanding gender difference. As you'll see in the following chapters, a lot of gender communication problems boil down to some simple differences between us both. Or at least that's the seed from which the problems grow. I didn't learn about these differences in books. They are things I've observed over and over again in my work. They are things you have all told me about yourselves. There are a lot of psychologists, neurologists, psychiatrists, anthropologists and others who see these differences too.

Until we understand each other's styles, we will keep misinterpreting each other. But that change starts with you. Until you understand how life looks in the shoes of the opposite sex, you will continue to misunderstand it.

The good news? At the end of your trip through these pages – through gender difference and back again – you'll see that while men and women are different, there's a lot more uniting you than dividing you. People basically want the same thing from their work: the feeling that they are contributing to a higher purpose and that they have the opportunity as individuals to learn and grow. You may not know that this is what you want, but as you're about to see, there are probably a lot of things you have yet to discover about yourself.

In the next chapter, you'll take the first step on the gender journey, and that means taking a good, hard look at how much you actually know about gender difference.

CHAPTER 2

How Gender Aware Are You?

Our resistance to generalizing or stereotyping propels us into a well-intentioned form of denial.

Carol Gilligan, Ph.D., author, *In A Different Voice*

How can you change the environment where you work? It sounds like a monumental task, but it starts with a pretty simple process: figuring out *your* role in the problem. To do that, first you have to take an honest look at your own level of 'gender awareness'. In other words, you have to face how much you actually know about how different the other sex is, versus how much you *think* you know. Trust me, we all carry around more assumptions and prejudices than we think we do. So get ready for some surprises.

Like many people who attend my workshops, you are probably thinking: 'This is a new millennium. We've made progress. Everyone agrees the sexes are equal. So what's the problem?' Or you may think, 'My mother and father lacked awareness about the differences between men and women but I don't.'

Most people come in to my workshops thinking there's no such thing as a gender issue any more, that there's no real problem to solve. It's only when they take the Gender Awareness Quiz that they start to change their minds. Men and women fall into one of four 'Stages of Awareness'.

The four stages are:

- Denial

- Recognition/ Awareness

- Confusion/Frustration

- Partnership/Congruence

Men's Stages of Awareness

The first quiz is for men. Consider this an opportunity to take a hard look at your own degree of awareness, without anyone criticizing or blaming you for how you think. The more honest you are about your feelings, the more you'll get out of it. Don't worry! It's not an end-of-term exam you have to pass. There's no passing or failing in gender difference. It's all about learning.

Questionnaire for men

How often do the following phrases run through your mind:

	Never	Some-times	Often
Time will take care of things.	☐	☐	☐
We've already employed more women.	☐	☐	☐
You have to be so politically correct these days.	☐	☐	☐

	Never	Some-times	Often
I treat everybody the same.	☐	☐	☐
We have the policies in place.	☐	☐	☐
I don't discriminate!	☐	☐	☐
It's the system; I can't change the system.	☐	☐	☐
Women just don't thrive in this environment.	☐	☐	☐
Women leave to have children.	☐	☐	☐
Women primarily leave due to 'work-life issues'.	☐	☐	☐
It's not about gender; it's about personality styles.	☐	☐	☐
It's a male-dominated environment.	☐	☐	☐
It's our company's culture.	☐	☐	☐
The system is totally oppressive.	☐	☐	☐
Equal opportunity will ensure fairness.	☐	☐	☐
It's the older generation who doesn't get it.	☐	☐	☐
This is not a place I want my daughter to work in.	☐	☐	☐
The work is tough; you have to be available 24/7.	☐	☐	☐

If you've answered 'sometimes' or 'often' to any of these statements, you are in Stage One or Stage Two of gender awareness. Don't get discouraged. The whole idea of this book is to bring you to the highest level, Stage Four. And when you get there, you'll not only be able to change your entire work environment, but you'll also love your job!

If none of these four Stages of Awareness is a perfect fit for you, don't worry. When you've read the descriptions of all of them, you'll understand where you stand. And nothing is written in stone. You may be in Stage One today and Stage Four tomorrow. Not everyone progresses one stage at a time, from One to Four. Some people skip a stage. Some people even move back a stage before they move forward.

Your job now is to examine the assumptions you carry around about women. You may not be conscious of it, but you have plenty of them. And women have them about you. Once you've taken your assumptions out of the closet and faced them you will be ready to move on to the next three chapters, where you will see how the other gender thinks and learn to really listen to what it is saying. Then you'll be ready for tools to improve your relations with the opposite sex in your work environment.

Stage One – Denial

There are two forms of denial. The first, 'Unaware Denial', is when you think you know something but, in fact, haven't the slightest clue. But there is also another, more sophisticated form of denial that can be more difficult to identify. I call it 'Enlightened Denial'. It happens when you think you know all there is to know about gender issues. Men in this form of denial have often made some superficial changes to their language or behaviour and think this is enough to do the trick.

Unaware Denial

Men in this first type of denial usually work in the male business environment, and are honestly convinced that women's experiences are the same as men's. These men don't think women's concerns warrant any special attention. They will say things like:

- 'We're all here to do a job and women should be treated exactly the same way as men.'

- 'Women say they're equal. I have to pay my dues. So should they!'

- 'Why should a woman get any special treatment?'

- 'Women shouldn't get something for nothing, and I won't give up what I've earned.'

Martin, a stockbroker working in London's financial district, made a typical denial remark. 'There's no gender issue at work. It's just different personalities. And you can't change people's personalities. If one of our brokers is having a bad day and gets a little out of line, why should that be such a big deal?' Other comments typical of men in denial are: 'We've got women. Our numbers are good,' and 'We've got policies for equal opportunity, work-life flexibility and harassment. There are no problems here.'

I heard a perfect example of this form of denial from a deputy minister who was arguing with a colleague about the principle of pay equity. 'Women get paid less than men because they *choose* to work in low-paying jobs!' he said. It was classic Stage One reasoning. 'They are the secondary income earner; we must be the breadwinners. . .'

Men in denial are comfortable with the working environment. They usually don't think there is such a thing as 'women's issues' in the workplace. 'We're all the same. We're all professionals,' they say. These men are often successful and in positions of power, or are heading in that direction. They don't see any reason for rocking the boat. On the contrary, they are quite satisfied with the status quo.

Enlightened Denial

Men in Enlightened Denial consider themselves 'beyond' gender issues. Younger men are often in this form of Stage One; they say things like:

- 'I know all about this gender stuff. I'm a modern guy. I don't discriminate.'

- 'The problem is the old guys.'

Men in Enlightened Denial often see successful women around them and conclude that the world has changed. 'The problem has been solved,' they say. As one U.S. colonel put it, 'We have two female colonels. They made it, so this problem is in the past!' While these men may have dealt with gender issues in their past, their attitude has resulted in a form of denial that closes doors to further discussion and presents a formidable obstacle to gaining understanding or increasing awareness of gender difference. Men in Enlightened Denial also believe gender problems can be solved simply by changing behaviour or language. They will decide to use the term 'women' instead of 'girls' or 'ladies'. They use 'he or she' in their sentences.

These men often have the best of intentions, but they tend to be stuck in rudimentary understanding of a few of the high-profile gender issues they hear about in the news.

Stage Two – Recognition/Awareness

Men in this stage realize that there is a fundamental difference in the way the world operates and is experienced by men and women. They want to fix it, but they don't know how. Men in this stage don't yet think it's necessary to change the status quo, and enjoy their 'male model' work environment. They will say:

- 'Really, I had no idea women felt that way.'

- 'I see the problem, but what can I do? It's the system. I can't change the system.'

- 'OK, just give me three things that I can do and I'll do them.'

Men often get into Stage Two when their assumptions have been challenged by an event in their personal lives. These men have often witnessed the experiences of a wife who starts or returns to a career, or of a daughter who enters the workforce, and they suddenly start seeing how the working world looks through a woman's eyes. They may see parallels between things their wife or daughter experiences and their own behaviour towards female colleagues. Hearing about public cases of discrimination against women can also push men into Stage Two. Such public cases include that of a woman at Deutsche Bank in the U.K. who in 2002 was forced to resign from her £300,000-a-year job because of her colleagues' sexist comments, and that of another woman at JP Morgan who was 'allowed to go', for asking to work family-friendly hours.

What happens when men hear of such cases? They can react in one of two ways. Some men in Stage Two can quickly revert back to Stage One because they feel forced to conform with a politically correct environment to avoid being sued; other men begin to confront their own conscious and unconscious assumptions about women.

Men in this stage have seen a problem and want to fix it. But these men do not see that that the status quo has to change. They still think things can continue in more or less the same way that they have in the past. Men in Stage Two usually don't stay there for long. Before they know it, they are struggling with Stage Three. 'OK, I get it: you keep saying that you feel like an outsider, but what can I do about it?' said a sincere police officer. This is a natural progression to the next stage.

Stage Three – Confusion/Frustration

Men in this stage recognize that the world occurs differently for women and men, but they feel as if they are being blamed for the misdeeds of all men throughout history. In Stage Two, they thought they had gender issues 'sorted out', but now they feel that they've tried everything and nothing has worked. They feel as though they are trapped in a no-win situation where they make endless concessions but get the same negative reactions from women. This can be a very frustating stage for men. Men in Stage Three say things like:

- 'We've made every effort, we have the policy, we built the business case.'

- 'I don't know what else we can do; maybe it's just the nature of the work.'

- 'We've already addressed this a long time ago; it's time to move on.'

Many men in companies that have had a hard time holding on to talented women turn to 'quick-fix' solutions, like a policy to hire more women. When these strategies flounder after a short period, men become frustrated and confused.

When that happens, men often slip back into a form of denial, saying things like, 'Maybe women just can't cope with it. We've tried to employ more women. We've had an equal opportunities policy in place for years. But the women keep leaving.'

As one senior manager at a major investment bank told me, 'There's nothing we can do. Women stay in personal and corporate banking, but not in investment banking. We're never going to change that!'

Ray, a mid-level manager at an electronic company was a typical Stage Three man. He said, 'Women can't make it in this company. Three years ago we had five women; now there's only one left. When the going gets tough, they just leave.' It's not just individual men who experience this stage. I deal with entire companies who are in Stage Three.

Richard, the chief executive officer of a famous investment firm, is a classic example of someone in Stage Three. 'We are losing ground with women,' he said. 'A few years ago our numbers looked fine, but we've slipped. We seem to either lose them altogether or they move to another side of the bank.' Richard was bitter after all his work to employ and promote women had failed. He was extremely frustrated, and found himself having a new kind of conversation with his colleagues. Instead of moving to Stage Four by recognizing the need to change the work environment, he reverted back to Stage One. 'Maybe it's just the nature of the beast! Maybe women just can't thrive in the investment side of our bank,' he said.

Stage Three can be so frustrating that men simply find it easier to revert back into the 'comfort zone' of Stage One. Or they might continue taking a stand and move on to Stage Four.

Stage Four – Partnership/Congruence

Men in Stage Four have recognized that women's experience in the workplace differs drastically from their own. They have stopped seeing women's issues as a zero-sum game and stopped trying to 'fix' gender issues just by changing their language and behaviour. Men in Stage Four don't say, 'Women's issues are something we have to put up with.' They have stopped seeing women as a class and see women's issues as people issues. They see that everyone can win when gender differences are recognized and understood. They say things like 'Hey, if we understand women better, everyone will benefit. I can personally continue my efforts in the workplace in a more inclusive and empowering way.'

Jim, a manager at IBM, had worked hard on achieving real gender awareness by actively changing the workplace environment within his department. 'This is not just the flavour of the month,' he said. 'We are going to make lasting positive changes around here!' He listened to both men and women, and collaborated on efforts to create win-win solutions. He could see how it had improved the working atmosphere and communication between his employees. It had even impacted on the many cultural difference that also existed. These benefits were reflected in a survey carried out by the human resources department. 'Everyone is doing a better job. The men are also seeing it as a positive change for them.'

Getting to Stage Four isn't always easy, as George, a director of a pharmaceutical company, told me. 'I had to struggle with the whole thing for a while without giving up,' he said, 'but I can clearly see the positive strides we have all made; we clearly enjoy working together more. Even the most difficult of tasks have become easier.' George obviously saw what needed to be done and implemented win-win ways of working together.

The key to Stage Four is 'ongoing commitment'. Men in this stage are ready to listen and keep listening. They have understood that the only way to learn is to get feedback from other people, from their closest women friends, their spouses or their colleagues. They have accepted that change is necessary. They are truly listening to what women have to say.

One particularly honest man in the onset of this stage admitted, 'I don't have a clue as to what it's like to be a woman!' He approached gender difference inquisitively, like a child, taking nothing for granted. It's a frustrating state to be in if you are trying to 'solve' something, but not if you are just trying to 'learn'.

Men, you might not go through Stage Three. Many men go straight from Stage Two to Stage Four. But Stage Two, the awareness stage, is particularly challenging. If you are in this stage you may find yourself using new information about gender difference simply to update old stereotypes. You end up with a sophisticated form of stereotyping. For instance, you may say, 'Women personalize things,' and then use this as an excuse for inaction, not as a tool for further understanding.

But men in Stage Four don't fall into that trap. They have achieved real partnerships with women. They are beyond just working on changing their attitudes and behaviour. You understand that women and men are equal, but not the same. You are aware that women have unique strengths and you know that when men and women share perspectives, it can be mutually empowering. You are comfortable with women's authentic style, and you are comfortable with your own authentic style.

You may think that Stage Four is an impossible ideal, but read on. In the next two chapters, you will probably find yourself spending time in all the Stages of Awareness. When you get to the end of this book, though, you'll be ready to experience Stage Four – and enjoying the benefits.

Women's Stages of Awareness

Women often think that it's men who don't know anything and who need to change. But nothing could be further from the truth! Women can be in denial too, and women's denial does the same damage as men's, provoking misunderstandings that feed misconceptions and leave everyone frustrated. Before you read about Women's Stages of Awareness, try this Gender Awareness Quiz to test your own assumptions and prejudices.

Questionnaire for women

How often do the following phrases run through your mind:

	Never	Some-times	Often
Time will take care of things.	☐	☐	☐
Men don't care.	☐	☐	☐
Men just don't understand.	☐	☐	☐
You have to challenge and confront the men.	☐	☐	☐
Women have to be more tough and demanding.	☐	☐	☐
Men wish for 'the good old days'.	☐	☐	☐
It's an 'old boys' club'.	☐	☐	☐
It's the system; I can't change the system.	☐	☐	☐
It's a male-dominated environment.	☐	☐	☐
What's wrong with a little swearing.	☐	☐	☐
It's not related to gender; it's personality styles.	☐	☐	☐
It's the corporate culture here.	☐	☐	☐
I'll just stick to doing my job and not worry.	☐	☐	☐
The system is totally oppressive.	☐	☐	☐
I'm not a feminist.	☐	☐	☐

If you've answered 'sometimes' or 'often' to any of these statements, you are in the lower levels of awareness. And now you'll see why.

Stage One – Denial/Unawareness

Women in this stage usually don't want to hear about gender difference. They equate the notion of being different from men with the notion of being weaker than men. Many women in Stage One have spent their lives trying to prove they are as good as, or better than, men in the workplace. They have shown they can make it on the same terms as men. To do this, they had to disprove stereotypes about women. They had to fight traditional attitudes among their co-workers. They attended leadership workshops where they were taught strategies like 'don't say excuse me', and 'boom your voice', and 'keep in control, make sure no one interrupts you, be the first to interrupt'. In other words, they learned to act like men.

Women in denial say:

- 'I don't see any specific challenges with gender.'

- 'I agree that we may have challenges, but they have to do with personality styles, and you can't change that!'

- 'Time is taking care of things.'

These women think the male model is 'just the way things are'. They don't imagine that things work differently, as in 'a different model'. Many women are in denial and are locked in a paradigm where being different is equated with being less – less capable, less talented, less appreciated, less successful. Women's differences have long been used as a justification for keeping them confined to the domestic sphere. Successful women are afraid that if they talk about difference, it will be used against them. 'I just want to leave that stuff behind and do my job,' they say. I've seen successful women go to great lengths to wipe out differences that might 'mark' them as women. One female politician actually had her assistant carry her handbag for her when she came to high-profile presentations! 'This is so I can march in just like men do!' she said.

Brenda, a powerful sales executive, told me, 'I'm not interested in putting this gender label on things. That's an excuse some women use. You just have to be like one of the boys!' Brenda was clearly a man in women's clothes; she had taken all the assertiveness and get-tough leadership training to fit in. But both men and women feared her. Women in this form of Stage One will say, 'I scratched and clawed my way up. Everyone has to go through it. Other women can't expect special treatment; they have to meet our criteria.'

Some younger women are in a different type of Stage One. At university, men and women are taught the same skills, in exactly the same way. So it's hard to discern the differences. Young women are convinced that young men are more or less like them, and that they will not act differently once they join the workplace. They haven't seen the patterns yet. When they experience patronizing behaviour from older male colleagues, they tell themselves it's just an exception to the rule, a relic from an older generation.

Women in this stage often call their work 'the treadmill'; they believe in 'sticking it out'. You just get up, go to work, and don't make too many waves.

Stage Two – Recognition/Awareness

Women in Stage Two, like men in Stage Two, recognize that there is a fundamental difference in how women and men perceive things, but don't yet want to change the status quo. They are prepared to continue working in the traditional hierarchical male structure without questioning or challenging it.

Surprisingly, although most women talk about the problems they have when working with men, they tend to believe deep down that their problems are somehow their own fault – that is, until they get to Stage Two. In Stage Two, women see and feel the challenges caused by gender difference. They discover that there is a larger cultural problem, and that many of their problems are not their own fault. Ann, a researcher at a pharmaceuticals company, told me, 'I used to think the problems I had at work were just my own fault. But after reading some research I talked to other women and now I see I'm really not alone.'

Women in this stage say:

- 'I thought I just had to work harder and prove myself more, but now I see that lots of other women feel the same way as I do.'

- 'Well, maybe there are gender differences, but I see them more at home than at work.'

- 'I just don't want to be labelled as the feminist or the complainer.'

Women in Stage Two have a sense of what's wrong, but they don't yet have the resolve to change things. They're not interested in challenging the way things are done. These women don't want to differentiate themselves too much from men. They are confident they can 'work around' the corporate structure. They are sure they will be able to find solutions on their own. 'I can cope with it,' they often say. They see feminist positions as 'extreme' so they don't join women's organisations in their company. 'Feminism doesn't really represent me or my voice,' they say.

Many women under thirty-five are in Stage Two. These women recognize the problems caused by gender difference, but like women in Stage One, they think time will resolve them. 'When the older men leave, things will improve,' they say. Many female service industry workers are also in Stage Two. They recognize there are differences in how men and women work, but their solution is to create a comfortable niche where they function well.

Stage Three – Confusion/Frustration

Women in Stage Three feel either forced to be resigned to their situation or they begin to plan an exit strategy. They may have made several attempts to deal with specific situations, but without tangible results. They say things like:

- 'I know what's wrong but everyone seems to tell me just to accept the way things are!'

- 'It's the system; you can only do so much.'

- 'I've tried to improve things on my own but that's the way things are.'

Many women in Stage Three have attained high positions within the existing corporate structure. They have experienced a great deal of stress trying to deal with gender issues in their workplace, and now they have just 'had it'. They are either ready to leave their jobs and do something else, or they 'leave and stay', just working their basic hours each day, without any enthusiasm, passion or commitment.

Women in Stage Three don't want to fight the system. Or they feel profound ambivalence about what to do, what their role should be, and whether or not they should be leading a revolution for change. They feel disempowered. Karen, a young black police officer, told me that new employees would eventually have to 'wake up and smell the coffee'. She said, 'That's just the way things are around here. The system is totally oppressive, but how am I supposed to take on the whole culture? I've been at this for 15 years and nothing has changed.'

Many women in Stage Three consider making a career shift

by starting their own business, or by looking for a smaller, more entrepreneurial company, where they are convinced the grass is greener. One Woman in Stage Three, who worked for a brewery, told me she was tired of the testosterone bouncing off the walls at her office. It seemed impossible to change the system. She was tired of trying to find her place in an environment that was male-centred. Like many women in Stage Three, she yearned for a job in which she could be herself, for an environment where she felt valued. She wanted to do something she felt made a difference.

Like Sandra at the law firm in Chapter 1, women who are firmly embedded in Stage Three usually choose to vote with their feet.

Stage Four – Partnership/Congruence

At the onset of Stage Four women have overcome the ambivalence they felt in Stage Three. They have seen that there is really no option. It's either the status quo or action, and they have decided to take action. Women in Stage Four have let go of the past and are focused on the future. They are starting from a clean slate. They have become 'intentional' and not 'reactive' about gender difference. They feel a sense of responsibility for their situation instead of a sense of resignation. They are willing to take a stand and work towards creating an inclusive environment at work. They say things like:

- 'The status quo doesn't have to last forever.'

- 'Now both men and women are making the effort, and we can all see the progress.'

- 'Instead of tolerating the differences, we are actually using our differences to our advantage.'

- 'I actually look forward to going to work now.'

Women in Stage Four are open to possible ways of improving their situation and they are interested in making the best of things. They experience a sense of empowerment and often join committees or initiate task forces on gender issues.

The risk in Stage Four? It can easily lead women back to Stage Three. Women's networks can often recreate the same kind of gender exclusion that women set out to change in the first place! Being proactive can lure women into an 'us versus them' mentality. I encourage women who have decided to take action to include men on their committees or task force. Some react by saying, 'What's wrong with just being a group of women?' When women react this way, it's a sign that they are in Stage Three, or slipping back to Stage Three. When women welcome my advice on inclusion, it means they are truly in Stage Four.

Later on in this stage women reap the benefits of their efforts to be inclusive. They have a sense of commonality, but they now understand the differences between women and men. Gender difference doesn't look like a 'problem to solve' any more. They see the advantages in men's and women's differences. They see both men's and women's potential strengths. They understand the potential of real partnership between men and women. 'There's power in our differences,' they say.

Women in Stage Four have left behind blame. They don't say, 'You don't understand' to the men around them, but say, 'Let's try to walk in each other's shoes for a while.' They understand that men and women often have different perceptions, and complementary strengths that can work together. Like men in Stage Four, women in Stage Four have progressed to the point of seeing gender differences as a win-win situation.

'It's a much nicer, richer way to get the job done!' said Anna, a bank executive in Stage Four, who had decided to take action. 'We are now really open to listening, communicating and resolving things as they come up! What a difference from when we used to take sides, and argue and debate about who was wrong and who was right! Better still, our results speak louder than words!'

What stage do most women tend to stay at? You probably guessed it – Stage Three. In that stage you have recognized there is a problem, but feel powerless to do anything about it. You are fixated on the problem, and will look for surveys and research to find evidence of how big the problem is. Or you try to 'do your bit' and end up frustrated and bitter. Then most women either revert to Stage Two or vote with their feet and leave. In other words, they are stuck in the problem identification stage.

How do you get past the problem identification stage? Read on. In the next chapter, I'll show you how men and women are different. Then I'll take you behind the scenes and let you listen to men and women talking honestly about what it feels like to work together. If you listen carefully, with an open mind – and put aside your assumptions – you'll see how differences create misunderstandings that leave everyone frustrated. You'll see how the spiral of misunderstanding gets started.

Then, once you've understood how gender difference creates misunderstandings and have learned to stand in the other sex's shoes, you'll be ready for the tools to overcome those misunderstandings and move to Stage Four.

CHAPTER 3

Where the Difference Starts

*Males and females have been a winning combination for 550
million years. The reason? Males keep their eye on one batch of
supremely important challenges and females keep their eye on
a totally different, but equally important, set of realities.*

Howard Bloom, author, *The Global Brain*

Remember Sandra, who left her job at the law firm, telling
her bosses she wanted to spend more time with her daughter?
That wasn't the real story. And when I met Sandra to talk
about why she had left, it all started to make sense.

Swimming in the water of the 'traditional business model',
Sandra had plenty of unique skills that she didn't feel were
being put to use, let alone valued. She had a real ability to read
people. She listened differently than her male colleagues did.
She read between the lines and caught things they didn't. She
saw the whole picture when they only saw part of it. She was
good at building relationships with clients and had a strong
ability to sense where people were coming from. Her clients
felt she was very tuned in to their needs. And they thought

she was thorough, taking her time to cover all the aspects of a problem before she came to conclusions.

Meanwhile, Nathan, at The Body Shop, also had some unique skills that he felt his female colleagues didn't see. Nathan was very task-oriented. He felt his colleagues meandered too much when they had meetings, jumping from one topic to another and taking too long to get to the point. Nathan was good at focusing, following a linear path of thinking and finding solutions to problems. Most of all, he thought he was good at getting things done, at moving from talk to action.

Nathan and Sandra's stories were no surprise to me. In this age of 'equal means the same', we systematically assume that differences in the way that people think, work and communicate are personality differences. But where men and women are concerned, nothing could be further from the truth. Men and women truly are two different kinds of fish. Like Sandra, most women excel in consensus building, relationship building, intuitive thinking and multi-tasking, to name but a few female skills. And most men share Nathan's linear thinking, and his task- and goal-oriented approach to work. These differences have nothing to do with individual personalities. Working men and women think, assimilate information and communicate differently.

The Scientific Evidence

Gender difference has not been a very popular topic of study in the scientific community until quite recently. It's no surprise why. By the early 1970s, women were pretty tired of hearing that they were biologically destined to take on the role of wife and mother. Society had decided that men and women were equal, and that women should be able to do the same work as men. Then a strange thing happened. Everyone started equating 'equal' with 'the same' and talking about gender difference became practically taboo.

By the 1980s, we once again recognized that there were real differences between men and women, but the debate was about how we got that way: nature or nurture? We were more interested in the answer to that question than in looking at what the actual differences were.

But at around that same time, something else happened. Technology and sophisticated research techniques allowed scientists to observe actual differences in the ways men and women's brains work. Scientists observed that men's brains were on average up to 10 per cent larger than women's. They also saw that certain parts of women's brains contained more nerve cells, and had significantly more neuron firings than men's brains did. Women's brains therefore have more connections for neuron firings, which are messages sent between various parts of the brain. In women's brains, for instance, the part of the brain associated with language skills contained up to 11 per cent more brain cells than the corresponding part in men's brains.

This was just the beginning. Throughout the 1980s and 1990s, scientists came to a wide consensus that men and women actually thought and processed information differently. Over the last decade, researchers in the fields of medicine, biology, sociology and psychology have built on these discoveries, showing us how men and women use their brains differently. For instance, women are stronger in verbal fluency skills, while men are stronger in spatial tasks. Women can remember lists of words or paragraphs better than men can. Men are better than women at mentally rotating images. Men are better at orienting themselves in a closed space and navigating themselves through a route. Yet women are better at recalling landmarks from a route.

Now that the taboo on talking about gender difference has lifted, gender difference has come out of the closet. It's amazing to hear what different professionals have to say about the differences they observe, and how early these start. Doctors say that gender differences of a baby can be observed within eight seconds of birth. One doctor told me he could even tell the differences if he was blindfolded!

Baby girls are more sensitive to touch, to light and to sounds. They are more easily comforted by soothing words and singing, and even before understanding language, girls are better than boys at identifying the emotional content of speech. Girls show greater interest early in life in communicating and reaching other people. They spend twice as long maintaining eye contact with a silent adult, and look longer than boys do at an adult who is talking. In a cradle, boys tend to talk to themselves, and are interested in toys and looking at abstract designs, like mobiles. Not only are baby boys less 'sensitive'; they also make less eye contact with their mothers. During the first months of their lives, boys have already developed a significantly shorter attention span.

Of course, anyone with children can see the differences between boys and girls as they grow older – especially when they are all thrown together in school. Sociologists have observed that even at a young age, little girls already have an inclination towards building relationships and building rapport with others. Girls seek to include newcomers in their groups, while boys are relatively indifferent to newcomers. Boys tend to be individualistic and competitive. They establish a pecking order in groups, and spend their time deciding who's better at what, rather than making sure everyone is included. Girls spend their time chatting in little groups while boys push each other around and make a lot of noise. It's as if girls live according to the slogan: 'We are together in this', while boys' motto is: 'Life is a contest'.

Some of the differences in how girls and boys act certainly may come from the way they are brought up. And they may be the result of evolution. After all, the human brain has been evolving for millions of years, according to the work men and women have been engaged in. In her book *The First Sex*, anthropologist Helen Fisher shows how men's brains evolved to make them able hunters, and women were gatherers. As hunters, men spent their time fighting to be 'at the top' while women spent theirs 'taking care'. Men's brains are adapted to focus on a goal, while women's brains take in a lot of stimulus – women had to look for food, build relationships around them and watch their children, all at once.

These writers' arguments confirm my own observations about how men and women think, act and communicate differently in the workplace. Evolution has certainly made men and women into two very different animals. But to understand how we differ, the discoveries of modern science excel in the way they enlighten us. Over the last decade, technological advances in the field of neuroscience have made it possible for scientists to virtually watch men and women's brains at work. And what have they discovered? Virtually every professional scientist and researcher who works in the field of gender has concluded that men and women's brains are different and that those differences influence almost everything we do.

We Have Different Brains

The human brain naturally makes a 'labour division' between the left and right sides. The right side of the brain controls language, delicate movements of the body and practical, orderly sequencing. The left side controls visual and spatial abilities, abstract thought and how we deal with our emotions. By tracking blood flow in the brain, scientists have been able to compare which parts of the brain men and women use for specific tasks. What they have found is that men use each side of the brain for specific tasks. But women use both sides of the brain almost equally, for lots of things.

According to Sandra Witelson, Professor of Psychiatry and Behavioral Neurosciences, McMaster University in Canada, who is studying Einstein's brain, 'The division of labor is not as distinct in women's brains'.[1] For instance, when men use language, the *right* side of their brain is active. When women use language, both hemispheres are active. When men and women process visual images, the same difference in labour division shows up. In women, both sides of the brain are busy 'seeing', while in men, only the *left* side is active. In experiments designed to test spatial ability, men almost exclusively used the right side of their brain, while women used both sides. When men and women are asked to identify the meanings of words, men use the left side of their brain while women, again, use both sides of their brain. Acoustic tests showed the same pattern. When women listen, their brain 'spreads the work out' across both sides of the brain, while men concentrate activity in one side at a time.

Looking for the root of why men and women use their brains differently to do the same tasks, researchers in the last few years have been looking at the 'corpus callosum' – a bundle of nerve connections between the two hemispheres of the brain. What they discovered was that the corpus callosum is proportionately larger in women's brains than in men's. Dr Roger Gorski, Professor of Anatomy and Cell Biology at the University of California in Los Angeles, says this supports the theory that 'in women, the two sides of the brain communicate more'. The study suggests that men are 'more dependent on one side of the brain than the other'.[2]

Researchers at the University of Pennsylvania made another interesting discovery. Tracking blood flow in the brain, they saw distinctly different patterns in men and women's brains. Dr Ruben Gur, the neuroscientist who led the study, asked men and women to perform different mental tasks. What he observed was that the men and women used different parts of their brains for similar tasks. Dr Gur also saw that compared to men's brains, women's brains were almost never 'off'. There was as much blood-flow activity in a resting woman's brains as there was in a thinking man's brain! 'The rate of neuron firing in women's brains is higher,' he explained.[3] Some scientists also believe that women's emotional centres are more widely distributed in the brain than men's, meaning they link emotions up to a lot of other brain processes.

This is how scientific brain differences come into play in our everyday lives – including the office.

We Really Do See Things Differently

It's as if men are looking at the world through binoculars, while women are looking at it through a kaleidoscope. I've often asked men and women what goes on in their minds when they walk into a room to sit down at a chair. Men say, 'I spot the chair and I go and sit down.' It's not that men *can't* see everything that's going on in a room. They just don't notice things automatically. Men tend to be more systematic and ritualized. Men get into a routine and stick to it.

Women notice lots of things on the way to the chair. In a matter of seconds, women notice the expressions on the faces of the other people in the room. They can gauge the mood in the room. They read the body language of those present. They notice where everyone is sitting. They can tell who's on board and who's not. Women make connections. It comes naturally to women, so naturally that lots of women aren't even aware they're doing it. Until they find out that men aren't!

There are two things going on here. As we have seen, women's brains never really rest, and the higher rate of communication taking place between the two sides of women's brains means they're making a lot of connections as they look around.

We Remember Different Things

Women's memory also plays a role in how women assimilate information. Studies on brain differences between men and women have shown that women store memory in more parts of their brains. Women notice many details and make instantaneous connections to things from the past. It all adds up to a kind of natural multi-tasking. Actually, it would make more sense to say that women excel in multi-thinking.

Lots of men have told me they think that women bring a lot of irrelevant stuff into things. Perhaps men should look at it differently. Women don't lack the ability to focus. They have the added ability to make a lot of connections between things. Women simply notice a lot of stuff men don't. There are times when the ability to focus quickly on the important features of a given problem is a valuable asset. As a way of assimilating information, it's neither better nor worse – just different. We have to get over the notion that there is only one way – the 'right way', to do a job. We need to get to a place where we appreciate and respect our different talents.

Men tend to see an isolated situation. They want to keep conversations to the point at hand. But because women have an interconnected memory, they have the ability to see patterns. For the men who are listening to them, it sometimes feels as though nothing is ever 'over'. Women just keep bringing stuff up.

We Solve Problems Differently

Women's brains naturally take a lot in. So it should come as no surprise that women go about solving problems differently than men do. Men tend to move quickly from problem to solution to action. Men see problems as things to tackle. They attack problems by isolating them, so they 'roll up their sleeves' and get down to work. For men, action is the imperative. Their instinctive impulse is to isolate, analyze and solve the specific situations referred to.

In comparison, women tend to juggle possible solutions before settling on one. Again, if it's true – as scientists tell us – that women use many parts of their brain at the same time, it's easy to see why women approach problem solving the way they do. Women apply multi-thinking to problem solving. They tend to explore all the angles first.

Of course, if men's brains naturally isolate activities, then it's easy to see why *they* go about problem solving the way they do! What I see in practice is that men see a problem, think of a solution and then act on it. They usually don't want to 'waste' time talking about it.

We Listen Differently

Even the way we listen is different. Simple laboratory tests have shown that men have difficulty filtering out background noises. When there is a lot of noise in the room, or if there are two or more conversations going on at the same time, men have trouble hearing what's being said to them. Women in the same situation get the message clear as a bell. Women have the ability to have a phone conversation and stay in tune with what is happening around them; for example, they are able to jot down notes on other things to do, while still being fully attentive on the phone. This is virtually impossible for men. Dr Ruben Gur says, 'Women often think men aren't listening, that they don't care. In reality, men just have more difficulty hearing what's being said to them.'

We Make Decisions Differently

The same patterns that we saw in problem solving show up in decision-making. The key difference in how men and women approach decision-making is in the perspectives each brings. For women, decision-making is first and foremost about visiting the entire context. Women tend to focus on the long-term implications of a decision. They make connections between one decision and another and wonder how one will affect another. Women wonder how a decision will affect the work of other departments, or the relationship they have built with a client. They instinctively connect the dots.

It doesn't usually occur to men to try to connect the dots when they are making decisions. When women do it, men usually appreciate it. But otherwise, men focus on the short term. The business world is a reactive place. Decisions have to be made and made fast. Men naturally tend to isolate issues in order to get to a decision as quickly as possible.

A former client of mine from General Motors described men and women's decision-making styles as a 'tree house'. It's as if women's preference is to go up in the tree house and look down on the whole scene!' he said, 'They want to explore the wider picture, how it all connects, while men just want to stay on the ground, or get down so they can do something. What I now find useful is to use both these strengths; it enhances our ability to make better and more thorough decisions. So now I actively seek that perspective out!'

We Prioritize Differently

Women's 'multi-thinking' really affects the way they go about setting priorities. Women are natural jugglers. A woman once described her office to me as a stove with twelve pots simmering all at once. 'They all need stirring at some point or another,' she said. The challenge for her was to keep her eye on each in order to see when it had to be stirred. Women tend to look at work and life in this way.

The juggling scenario can be tough for men to deal with. Men tend to approach priorities by dealing with things one at a time and crossing them off a list. Men say, 'I select the most important pot and give it a stir, then move on to the next one.'

We Feel Emotions Differently

Brain differences also mean we feel things differently. McMaster University psychologist Sandra Witelson discovered that men and women respond differently to emotional information fed to the right and then the left hemisphere.[4] In men, the emotional functions are concentrated in the right side of the brain, while women's emotional responses are located in both the left and the right side of the brain. Since the two sides of men's brains are not as well connected as women's, men have more difficulty expressing their emotions. A man keeps his emotions in the right side, while the power to express speech lies over on the left side. So in men, the information just doesn't flow as easily from the emotional right side of the brain to the verbal left side of the brain.

Women do not have this separation because of the way the female brain is organized. The result is that women are less able to separate emotion from reason.

When the accounting firm Deloitte & Touche, in collaboration with the Fortune Marketing Research Group, surveyed hundreds of executive businessmen and women about the skills they thought women needed to acquire to be more effective in business, the executives responded with several suggestions. These included: women should learn to separate their emotions from their business decisions and take things less personally.[5] Now you know why this is hard for women to do.

Continuing this observation, anthrolopoligst Dr Helen Fisher, author of *The First Sex*, says women have a propensity to personalize things because the emotional connectors in the brain are more linked to the verbal.[6] Women express their emotions through verbal means. This is not to say that men don't feel emotions; it's just harder for men to express them through verbal means.

We Read Emotions Differently

It is always helpful to know if a person is happy, sad, interested or bored. However, tests show that men have more difficulty than women in deciphering facial expressions. In particular, men have more difficulty understanding what a certain facial expression means on a woman's face than on a man's. Tests also show that women's brains simply do not work as hard as men's do when they are identifying facial expressions. In other words, compared to men, women identify people's emotions without even trying.

Dr Gur, at the University of Pennsylvania, has carried out some well-documented research in this area. He performed a test where he showed pictures of men and women smiling, frowning and crying. When he asked men to read the faces, most of them could identify the correct emotion on the men's faces but often had trouble reading the women's faces. Women easily read the emotion on both the men's and the women's faces.[7]

Emotions are often the first thing women notice. They read emotions even before they listen to what people say. For men, 'I'm doing fine,' means 'I'm doing fine,' even if the person who says it is frowning. For women, it's the frown that counts.

We Deal with Stress Differently

Women and men respond differently to stress. To deal with stress, men either fight or withdraw and go into hiding to focus on the problem. Women tend to react to stress by sharing their feelings. They turn to their friends.

Two women professors at the University of California in Los Angeles made a groundbreaking study about stress recently. Scientists have long believed that stress releases hormones that prompt the body to either stand and fight or flee as fast as possible. They long assumed the fight-or-flight instinct was the same in men and women. As Dr Laura Cousino Klein, one of the two women scientists, explained, 'We were talking one day in a lab about the joke that when the women who worked in the lab were stressed, they came in, cleaned the lab, had coffee, and bonded. When the men were stressed, they went off somewhere to be on their own.'

Dr Klein and her colleague decided to test the idea that women reacted differently to stress. They discovered that when women are stressed, they release a hormone called oxytocin, which buffers the fight-or-flight response, probably to ensure that women tend to their children and gather with other women instead of running away from danger. When women engage in this tending or befriending reflex, studies suggest that more oxytocin is released, which further counters stress and produces a calming effect. This calming response does not occur in men, says Dr Klein, because testosterone, which men produce in high levels when they're under stress, seems to reduce the effects of oxytocin. According to Dr Klein, oestrogen enhances it. This difference between men and women has huge repercussions in our everyday lives.[8]

We Work Differently in Teams

Women are natural collaborators, whereas men naturally compete and want to win.

A group of researchers based at Emory University in Atlanta, Georgia watched men's and women's brains while they played games. The researchers tested the women on a board game, while scanning their brains with an MRI scanner (watching the blood flow). The blood activity in the reward centres of the women's brains showed that these centres were activated when the women collaborated; the more they collaborated, the more the reward centres were activated. The researchers discovered that when women are involved in a situation where they are cooperating with someone else, they experience activation in brain areas that are also activated by 'rewards' such as food, money and drugs. This indicates that women's bodies may have been somehow pro-grammed to label 'cooperation' as 'rewarding'.[9] Other researchers have found that women's brains register collaborating as a reward, even when collaboration isn't in a particular woman's own self-interest. Men feel reward by beating the competition and win-ning the game. In teams, they feel reward by being the star of the team, or the team leader.

It's No One's Fault. We're Just Different

When I present what scientists say about gender difference to my workshop participants, it comes as a big relief to everyone, men and women alike. Why? Gender difference is no one's fault. No one should feel guilty or deficient because of the way he or she thinks or processes emotions. Men and women's brains work dif-ferently and you can't change that. All these years we have been blaming the other sex for not 'thinking' in the same way that we do, but it's not their fault. Men and women don't think the same way. They don't see the same reality the same way. They really are very different from each other.

In my twenty years of work in the gender field, the patterns I've noticed are absolutely consistent with what scientists say about gender difference, from women's more 'highly connected' brains to men's more 'focused' approach to problem solving. In every company I've worked with, these differences have provoked innumerable misunderstandings, conflicts and hurt feelings.

Here's a brief summary of the different approaches of men and women:

Women	Men
Justify.	Carry on regardless.
Look for areas of agreement.	Look for gaps.
Bond in conversations.	Bond in games and tasks.
Are validated in relationships.	Are validated in accomplishments.
Are multi-thinkers – switch topics in coversation.	Are linear thinkers, dealing with one problem at a time.
Have multi-dimensional insights.	Have linear insights.
Are concerned with feeling connected.	Are concerned with independence.
Usually explore every detail before concluding.	Usually want to get straight to the point.
Share problems when they want to talk about them.	Share problems only when they want them fixed.
First see a problem as 'their' problem.	First see a problem as someone else's.
Have personal breakthroughs through validation.	Have personal break-throughs through struggle and debate.

It's no accident that men and women approach the same situations or tasks so differently. Men and women *are* different. Their processes for assimilating information, for thought and for communication, are all different. This creates all sorts of misunderstandings. Why? As you're about to see in the next two chapters, men and women assume that the other sex thinks exactly like they do. So when a member of the other sex doesn't react in the way that you would, you jump to conclusions about what they mean.

Seeing how men and women's brains differ physiologically is just the start. In the next two chapters, you'll see how those differences translate in the real world. You'll hear men and women talk openly about how it feels to work together and start to see how gender differences create misunderstandings, which feed more misunderstandings and leave both men and women frustrated.

But there is light at the end of the tunnel. You'll see how you contribute to gender-based misunderstandings, and that's the first step in learning how to resolve them.

CHAPTER 4

Men's Challenges and Women's Insights

You have to look at things from two points of view, he explained, to really understand it. The approach is to help us all understand the conversation we find ourselves in and gain insights from each other, not label one way right and the other wrong and thereby further drive a wedge between the sexes.

Neils Bohr, Danish physicist

It's amazing how little men and women know about one another. I mean, *really* know about one another. Men and women think they know a lot about the opposite sex, but in fact, what they have are a lot of opinions. Opinions are fine. But they're limited in scope, substance and usefulness. Why? Because we get opinions from mapping others' behaviour on to our own experience.

When we rely on opinions to judge the other sex's behaviour, we tend to look for confirmation of what we already believe. We also tend to decide instinctively whether other people are 'right' or 'wrong' instead of really listening to them.

Opinions are good for making more opinions. But they're not very good tools for learning. In this chapter, the time has come to put aside your opinions. What you're about to receive are insights. Insights are discoveries we make when we become aware of something that we weren't previously conscious of. They are about discovery, about alerting your mind to something entirely new, about grappling with something you never really thought about before, about taking a look at the world through an entirely different pair of eyes. Few of us are paid to have insights, so we don't think about them very much. But insights are exactly what we need to understand the other gender. They are the moment we say, 'Ah-hah!'

At the beginning of my gender workshops, I divide up the men and women and send them into separate rooms so both men and women can talk freely about what's really on their minds without worrying about how to put things. This chapter is about what goes on in the men's room – what the men say, and the conclusions they come up with. Men, you will relate to many of the comments you are about to read. And women, you will get a chance to stand in the men's shoes. This is your first chance to get some 'Ah-hahs' about men. But you'll only be able to do that if you put aside your opinions and really listen.

Many women think they understand men through and through. When women hear men's challenges they are tempted to trivialize and dismiss them. It's easy to label men and dismiss them as dinosaurs. Try to resist. Take this information at face value, for what it is. I have heard literally tens of thousands of men talk about the same challenges over and over again. Men truly feel the way they say they do. Women, try to imagine how you would act if you went to work every day with men's concerns. If learning is what you want, then look for insights. Men are giving you the chance to see how the world works from their own perspective. Why not take them up on their offer?

Like I said, it's amazing to see how little men and women know about each other. The proof? When women hear men's challenges, their most common reaction is: 'I never realised men felt that way.'

Men's Top Five Challenges Working with Women

It's difficult to get men to talk about what it feels like to work with women. When I ask the men about their challenges, many close up. 'There are no problems,' they say. One of my male associate facilitators explains men's reaction this way:

> Men are very, very careful about when they talk about women. Sometimes it takes a good five minutes of silence before anyone speaks up. They're concerned about being accused of not being politically correct. When they do start to talk, they say things like, 'Don't write this down . . . You can't put it that way!' They're very concerned about having this conversation. It's uncomfortable for them.

For women, this alone should provide you with a huge insight into the male perspective on the gender issue. Most women are convinced that men aren't interested in talking about the gender issue. Women think men are resisting. In fact, men are rather intimidated by the question. Not many women would imagine that the all-powerful male in business would feel you needed to be so cautious when talking about women. But you are, and we'll soon see why.

These are some of the typical things men say inside the men's room. If you are a man, feel free to tick off each challenge you can relate to.

☐ Men feel they have to be careful.

☐ Men feel confused.

☐ Men fear harassment charges.

☐ Men feel reverse discrimination.

☐ Men feel blamed.

Challenge 1 – Men Feel They Have to be Careful

Men say:

- 'I feel as if I'm walking on eggshells around women.'

- 'If I don't know a particular woman, I have to be even more attentive, more cautious. I just don't know how she's going to react!'

- 'I want to be respectful but sometimes it blows up in my face.'

Many men feel they always have to be a little on guard with women. They don't know how women will react in situations in which men's reactions are predictable. As one lawyer told me, 'If my colleague Harry does a bad job in court one day, I can just tell him, "Harry, you did a lousy job in there today," and we move on. With a female colleague I just never know. I mean, I feel that I have to massage in criticism to slowly get her to get the point. Why? Because I know she'll take it personally. Harry will just shrug it off.'

Time and again, men report that:

- They feel that women remember everything, and that they have to be so careful, because 'things come back to haunt you years after it happened'.

- They feel that women take things personally and overreact to things that they themselves would just shrug off.

- They worry about how to deliver criticism to female colleagues without offending them.

- They just don't know where women are coming from.

- They fear women will think they are being condescending or discriminating if they 'take them under their wing'.

- They don't know whether to compliment a woman on her appearance or not. On the one hand, it seems like a courteous thing to do. But then she might take it the wrong way.

- They are afraid of women crying!

Women's Reaction

Women are always surprised to learn that men spend so much time thinking about these things. And they are amazed at how afraid men are of making women cry. As one women put it, 'I had no idea how concerned men were about how to act with women, how to make good impressions on women, how to avoid offending women. I just thought men never thought about it.'

Of course, it's not all roses. Women get a little depressed when they hear men talk about being careful with them because in a way it confirms their worst fears. Women hear old clichés at work. 'What's this business about being afraid of making us cry?' they ask. 'How many times have you seen a woman cry at work?' Women hear men implying that all women are the same and that men can't afford to be direct with any of them.

The insight for women Women aren't happy to hear that men really *do* treat them cautiously. But when men talk about how careful they feel they need to be with women, they see that what they thought was dismissive behaviour is, in fact, just hesitant. This is one of women's first 'Ah-hah!' moments. They realize that when men seem to be brushing them off, they are really just being careful. And the reason they are being careful? They sincerely don't know what the rules are. They don't know how women will react to what they say and do, and they are afraid to offend, or to be misunderstood. So men often act in ways that make it possible to steer clear of problems, conflicts and friction with women, and just try to find ways of avoiding these things. Women should understand that men's caution is not intended, but that it really is a big challenge. They should let men know that there is no need to be cautious with them, and then should share their insight that they understand the way men feel.

The insight for men Men see that when they hesitate with women and try to avoid problems by skirting around issues, women feel they are being dismissed. And that's the main reason why women react negatively to things. To solve this, men should just try being as direct as possible with women, even to the point of telling them that they are afraid of their reaction. Women will welcome this approach. To them, it will resonate as honest and considerate.

Challenge 2 – Men Feel Confused

Men say:

- 'I wish I knew the ground rules with women; do I call you "women"?, "ladies"?, "girls"?, "guys"?'

- 'Do I pull out the chair for women or don't I?'

- 'Is it OK to talk to women about their families at work?'

Most men are working in a hierarchical 'male' work paradigm, but the rules are changing, and men know it. That leaves most men confused. Lots of men say they were brought up to show respect for women, but when this aspect of their upbringing comes to the surface, they get mixed signals from women. This leaves men wondering what they're supposed to do.

One young engineer told me the story of a scene he witnessed between two colleagues: 'I watched this team from our office come out of the lift after a tough meeting. A senior bloke put his hand on one of the women's shoulders and congratulated her for her good work and she snapped back, "From the elbow down please!" I mean, I was shocked that she would have that kind of reaction when the bloke really meant well. Personally, I try to be helpful and courteous and treat women the same way I would treat men. It's not condescending. But some women get it and others don't. The rules seem to vary from woman to woman and even from day to day. I can't seem to get the ground rules down!'

Over and over again, men report that:

- They were brought up to be polite and considerate to women, but get mixed signals from them when they behave that way.

- What they learned from their mother, sister or spouse doesn't seem to apply with their female colleagues.

- They want to help women out by, say, offering them a ride home, but are afraid they'll seem like they're coming on to them.

- They don't know how physical contact will be interpreted.

- They feel that they have to be on guard when it comes to dealing with women.

Women's Reaction

Women see that men's trepidation is real. They don't yet understand why men are so confused, but they see that the confusion is real. It's often a relief for women: they have always sensed men's uncertainty around them and wondered what was behind it.

Women don't understand that what men are telling them is that when they deal with other men at work, the rules and procedures are fairly simple: when men are together there are certain norms and expectations and everyone just follows them. Lots of men wonder whether these 'men's rules' are still appropriate in the workplace, but between men, they work, and they supply men with a comfort zone.

Men say they don't spend a lot of time thinking about things like 'how to deliver the message' to other men, but women may not be aware of men saying that when they're dealing with women, this communication process becomes much more complicated. They get different reactions from different women in different situations – or even from the same women. This leaves men confused and desperately searching for a set of rules they can apply whenever they are dealing with women.

The insight for women When men are confused about the rules of how to act with women, or how to communicate things to women, they often end up not saying what they mean for fear of being misunderstood. That solves one problem, but creates another: it makes women feel excluded. When men act reluctant, or hesitant, women feel as though they are being left out of the loop or pushed out of inner circles where decisions are being made. Women have to realize that this is not intended. When asking questions, for example, women should put them in an open-ended and non-blaming way so that they feel included. And as we'll see later, being included is what women report as one of their main challenges in dealing with men!

The insight for men There is no single set of rules for working with women. As soon as you start to apply a single set of rules, women will sense it and they won't like it. Instead, men should try to deal with women as they would with a client: have your antennae up; be constantly aware and looking for feedback. Engage, be interested and ask for information. As you read on about women's challenges and understand how women are 'different fish', it will become easier to figure out how to act.

Challenge 3 – Men Fear Being Accused of Harassment

Men say:

- 'I won't even go to lunch with a woman any more.'

- 'Do I ask her out for dinner when we are working late? No way!'

- 'I'm even worried when I'm alone in a lift with a woman.'

Men are very concerned about being accused of harassment and terrified of false allegations. As one man put it, 'I've seen what one of my colleagues went through when he was accused of harassing a female colleague. I know for a fact he wasn't, but the company crucified him.' Because of what they've seen happening around them, men are determined to do everything they can to avoid any accusations – to the point of not even commenting on a female colleague's new haircut. Men are afraid that since they don't know what the rules are, they could do something as a friendly gesture that women would misconstrue as harassment.

It's hard to overestimate the fear men have of being falsely accused of harassment. Men have seen it or heard about it and are convinced that there's nothing as career limiting as being labelled a harasser. Even the suggestion that someone is *contemplating* bringing an action against them frightens men.

Women's Reaction

Women are always surprised to find out how worried men are about harassment. This may come as a surprise to men, but women don't actually spend a lot of time worrying about the possibility of harassment (unless, of course, they have actually been harassed, in which case it becomes a very real concern). Women say they had no idea that men felt this way, or that the men that they thought they had built a good relationship with still shared this concern. As one woman put it, 'To me it's pretty simple to see when it's harassment and when it's not.'

The insight for women When men fear harassment charges it also results in them holding back on relating to women, and women now see that they can easily assume that this is because a man doesn't care, or is disinterested or distant. But, in fact, men do care; they just don't know how to show it any more. Women should understand the degree to which this fear is a concern – it's absolutely impossible to trivialize. There is no easy answer as to what women should do. You have to build relationships, and build the level of trust so men feel safe.

The insight for men Men are surprised to find out that women don't really spend much time thinking about harassment. My advice to them? Don't hold back in your relationships with women. Do your homework (as you would with a client) and think things through. Women will always welcome a well-framed compliment. But if you hold back too much, the fun and humour at the office will quickly disappear. And when that happens, everyone loses.

Challenge 4 – Men Perceive Reverse Discrimination

Men say:

- 'I see some job ads and just think that white male need not apply.'

- 'I think the best candidate should get the job, not the best woman candidate, but that doesn't seem to be the way the world works these days.'

- 'I saw a woman become chief executive officer without any operational experience! Are you going to try to tell me it wasn't just because she's a woman?'

Some men believe that the white male is slipping further and further down the corporate ladder. Statistics may not support men's feelings that white males are being systematically passed over for the best jobs, but individual and anecdotal experiences are still feeding their pessimism. Many men take a look at their future and come to the conclusion that because of equal opportunities policies, men's options are limited.

The men who already have established careers don't feel they're free from reverse discrimination either. As one man told me: 'There's all this stuff out there for women – networks and clubs for women only, special interest groups for professional women. If I belonged to a club for men only, people would say it was chauvinism.'

On a closely related theme, many men bring up the problem of double standards that favour women. 'Women can crack dirty jokes about men now and it's considered perfectly acceptable,' they tell me. There is also a feeling that men (and incidéntally, women without children) are still expected to work harder than women with children. 'Nobody questions it when a woman has to leave early to take care of her children or something, but I'm still expected to be there,' one man told me.

Women's Reaction

Most women think reverse discrimination is a myth. They know that some men believe that women are being promoted because they're women, that there's more focus on women in the workplace than on men, and that qualified men are being overlooked because of this. But this doesn't cut any ice with women – particularly those who work in non-traditional fields and constantly feel that they have to struggle to get taken seriously.

The insight for women I encourage women to put these feelings aside when they listen to men talk about reverse discrimination. Many men do genuinely feel that reverse discrimination is working against them. And that perception affects men's behaviour towards women. Whether, statistically, reverse discrimination exists, or is justified if it does, is not the point. When men feel reverse discrimination, they react with a kind of cynical defeatist attitude. They say things like, 'She'll get the job anyway, because she's a woman. So why should I bother.' They're only talking about their own feelings, but they inadvertently reinforce one of women's Top Challenges: women's fear of being a 'token'. This reaction, in turn, feeds women's feeling that they are being tested all the time.

Again, recognize that men's perception is real for them. Women should encourage men to validate their perceptions. Ask for specific statistics which prove that the perception is a reality, and soon men will see that it's not a reality, but a myth. Tell men that, even today, it remains a perception and not a reality. But be careful not to blame individual men for their perceptions.

The insight for men While employment equal opportunities policies are a reality, reverse discrimination is a myth. Men should avoid generalizing, using just one scenario of a woman who moved up a few levels too quickly. What equal opportunities policies have done is to force employers to be more objective in their decisions. They have to justify their choices now. Traditionally, men have been employed for their potential, while women tend to be employed for their track record and proven skills. Equal opportunities means everyone has to be employed according to the same criteria.

Challenge 5 – Men Feel Blamed

Men say:

- 'When I hear the words "male-dominated workplace", it just sounds like feminist male-bashing to me.'

- 'Why do women blame all men for the historical mistakes of a few?'

- 'I feel as though I have to apologize for being a man these days.'

Many men feel they have been tarred with the same wide brush courtesy of the feminist movement and that women lump them together in one pile. 'We're never treated as individuals,' men tell me. 'Just because your boss mistreated you 15 years ago, doesn't mean it's my fault.' They feel that the media and corporate culture has encouraged an anti-male way of thinking, and it has infiltrated all domains of their lives. This puts men automatically on the defensive. Every time they hear the words 'male dominated', they feel as if they're being blamed for something they had no control over.

'I feel blamed for breathing,' they tell me. 'I feel that I'm damned if I do and damned if I don't.'

Women's Reaction

Here, the lights really start going on for women. Most women have witnessed or participated in, or even initiated, some male-bashing at work, and they know it. In a world where the power balance has traditionally favoured men, women feel justified in such behaviour. It seems normal, even acceptable these days to take a stab at men, all in good humour. Some women, particularly the older ones, even make more jokes when men present this challenge. 'But you ARE wrong!' they say.

Now women see that comments like these don't appear as harmless to men. They see that even if women consider that sort of behaviour harmless and acceptable, men don't. Men feel blamed for being men. Women are always surprised to find this out. What women consider a sort of teasing equates to men as 'blaming me for breathing'. There's a glimmer of light appearing though, as women step out of their shoes and start to look at their own behaviour from a man's perspective.

The insight for women When men feel they are being tarred with the same brush, they often react with a kind of dismissive or even cynical behaviour towards women. Many men act this way without even realizing it. But women hear the message. It reinforces some of their top challenges, as you will see in the next chapter: the feeling that they are dismissed, excluded and tested. Nevertheless, women should avoid making sweeping generalizations about men, avoid saying 'all men are', and treat men as individuals that are at different Stages of Awareness.

The insight for men Men need to speak up and challenge women when they feel they are being blamed for being men. Women do have a tendency to see patterns and speak globally about men when they feel they are victims of discrimination. Men should take a stand on this one. They should tell women they feel that they're being unfairly blamed (without blaming women in return!).

It might be interesting for both male and female readers to know that the 'challenges' men present are almost always the same. Year after year, men always say the same things about working with women and women say the same things about working with men. It doesn't matter if they are lawyers or accountants, secretaries or soldiers, middle managers, chief executive officers, office workers or the semi-retired, middle-aged or thirty-somethings. The same themes come up, over and over again.

So is it true? Are men really getting the short end of the stick in the working world? Are the new rules really working against them?

The only 'truth' I'm really interested in is men's feelings and how these interact with the feelings of women. After listening to thousands of men talk about what it feels like to work with women, I can say with absolute certainty that they really do feel this way. Men really are confused and they do feel that they have to be cautious when they're dealing with women. They really do feel they are being unfairly blamed for the way chauvinists have acted in the past, and they really do feel that they are paying the price by being victims of a policy of reverse discrimination. Women might not like what they hear, but they have to accept that it is an accurate picture of how many men feel. And of course, women should listen to men – because men's challenges shed light on a lot of the behaviour that women misinterpret as dismissive and exclusionary.

You are listening to the voices of 25,000 men who have all said the same things about what it feels like to work with women: what worries them, what confuses them and what leaves them perplexed. This is not about who's right and who's wrong. You'll soon see why.

Many women who are reading this are probably wondering, 'Then what should I do?' My advice? Read on.

But first, women, it's your turn to talk. And men, it's time for you to listen.

CHAPTER 5

Women's Challenges and Men's Insights

The mind, once stretched by a new insight, never regains its original dimensions.

O.W. Holmes, author, *The Poet at the Breakfast Table*

I started the chapter on men's challenges with a warning for women to avoid judging men too quickly. 'Look for insights,' I said. When women really listen to men talking about the challenges they face when working with women, they are often amazed by what they hear.

This chapter starts with a similar warning to men. Men: try to resist arguing with women. When men listen to the women's challenges, they tend to hear women's stories as isolated incidents and react by saying, 'That only happened that one time. It didn't mean anything.' They particularize each point, challenging what women say, rather than trying to understand women's point of view.

Well, men, the fact of the matter is that when women talk about their challenges, they are not talking about individual incidents. I often use the expression 'water torture' to illustrate how many women feel. When they talk about individual incidents to

illustrate what they mean, what they're really saying is how discouraged they are by the build-up of similar incidents. The drip,
drip, drip effect of repeated experiences really gets to women.

A woman's boss calls her 'sweetie' or 'dear'. It may not be a
big deal on its own, but when she's heard it continually from different male colleagues over the years it starts to wear her down.
The press calls Tony Blair's senior female colleagues 'Blair Babes'.
George Bush calls his senior female colleagues 'My Moms'. It's
easy for men to particularize and challenge these kinds of complaint, but women have heard it all before, and they're sick of it.

My advice to men on this issue is the same as my advice to
women. Forget about who's right and who's wrong. Resist the
temptation to disprove what the opposite sex is saying. Put aside
your opinions, the ideas you already have and the judgements
you've formed based on past experiences, and look for those 'Ah-
hah' moments that tell you you're learning something new. I've
heard 25,000 women say the same thing and raise the same complaints over and over again, from year to year, from profession
to profession. There's got to be something in it.

And finally men, remember you are getting a rare opportunity to go behind closed doors and listen to what women say
when you're not around. You're about to see how women feel at
work. Consider this an opportunity to put yourself in women's
shoes.

Women's Top Five Challenges Working with Men

Interestingly, when I ask women about the challenges they experience when working with men, there are always a few women
who put up their hands and declare: 'There's no difference between
women and men.' They say, 'Problems at work aren't because of
gender,' or 'Gender has nothing to do with it; it's individual

personalities.' Curiously, it's usually the youngest women who make those claims. When the older women hear this, they often nod their heads and say, 'You just haven't been working with men long enough. You'll see.'

With the odd exception, though, most women have plenty to say about what it feels like to work with men. It's as if women have been harbouring these thoughts for years but have never had the chance to voice them. There is no dead air in the women's room. And that's not the only difference from the men's room. While the men tend to challenge each other until they decide who's right, women always treat the brainstorming session as a team effort. They instinctively turn the exercise into a collaborative process, sharing experiences with one another and building on them. As the first women start to talk, the other women acknowledge them with 'uh-huhs', then reinforce their ideas with their own perspective, effectively building a list. It's not unusual for women to come up with ten or twelve pages of challenges, while men come up with only one or two.

One thing that still surprises me about women is how shocked so many of them are to find out that other women share their feelings about working with men. Amazing as it sounds, women may talk a lot together about the men they work with but rarely share their deepest personal feelings about the subject. It's easy to talk about what men are and how men act, but harder to talk about how their behaviour makes you feel. Women, think back to the many times you've talked to your female colleagues about men, and you'll see this is probably true for you too. Women rarely talk together about how men's behaviour affects them – particularly as they rise through the ranks and have to be more cautious about revealing the problems they may be experiencing.

Why do many women keep their real feelings to themselves? Strangely, it's because deep down, they suspect it's their own fault. It all boils down to the way many women internalize the problems they experience at work. Internalizing means looking for the answers to a problem in your own behaviour, and women do this all the time. When women have problems working with men, they may tell other women it's a particular man's fault, but instinctively, they wonder whether *they themselves* played a role in creating the problem. They tend to assume it's their own fault. It's very subtle. Most women don't know they're doing it.

When women hear other women articulate exactly what they've been thinking for years, their faces light up. Your face will probably light up too! Many women have lived through decades of gender-based communications problems wondering, 'What's wrong with me?' They are just amazed when they find out that other women struggle with the same problems and feel exactly the same way as they do about working with men.

As in the case of the men, my workshop often provides the first formal opportunity for women to speak openly about what it's like to work with the other gender. These are the kinds of things they say. If you are a woman, feel free to tick off the challenges you relate to.

- [ ] Women feel dismissed.
- [ ] Women feel excluded.
- [ ] Women feel tested.
- [ ] Women feel they have to be like men.
- [ ] Women feel tokenism.

Challenge 1 – Women Feel Dismissed

Women say:

- 'Men don't seek my opinion, or if they do, they ignore it.'

- 'Men talk a lot but they don't listen.'

- 'My boss treats me like his daughter!'

Women often feel their words somehow don't have the same weight as the words spoken by their male counterparts. Many women tell me about experiences at meetings where they made an important point or came up with a new idea only to have it ignored. But when the same point was later picked up by a male co-worker, everyone listened. 'Men only seem to listen to men, no matter what we say,' they tell me. When these women try to explore an issue by talking about various aspects of a problem, they feel that men shut them out, and that they are being dismissed and discounted.

Many women also feel that old stereotypes about women are preventing men from listening to them. 'When I bring up ideas and remind my male colleagues of past discussions they tell me I'm nagging,' says one woman.

Women say:

- 'When we make points at meetings, we get passed over. Then a man takes the point up and says more or less the same thing and everyone gives him three cheers. It's as though we're not there.'

- 'When I try to talk through problems at work I just get grunts from men. It's as though men just want to get to the bottom line and get on to something else, as fast as possible.'

- 'When I bring up sensitive issues, no one listens to me. Then I keep bringing up the points again and get accused of nagging. It always gets attributed to my gender. Did you ever hear a bloke say that another bloke was nagging? They say he was forceful!'

- 'The tone changes when we enter a room full of men and men's behaviour changes, their body language shifts, their language alters and the mood changes.'

Men's Reaction

When they hear women say they feel dismissed, men's first reaction is to map women's feelings onto their own experience. They come up with the inevitable conclusion: 'Sometimes I feel dismissed too. So what?' They usually pursue this line of reasoning by challenging women, picking apart the examples women give and asking for more proof.

The insight for men While the men are arguing over whether women's complaints are legitimate or not, something interesting usually happens. One man has a flash of insight and speaks up. 'Listen chaps. Look what we're doing. We won't let the women get a word in edgeways because we're so busy talking among ourselves and arguing with everything they say. *We're dismissing them!*'

The men usually get it. It's their first, 'Ah-hah'.

Now that you understand this challenge for women, listen actively, even when you feel they may be digressing; understand that what they're saying may be relevant. If you have trouble following their train of thought, try and clarify things in your mind by reflecting back on what you've heard.

The insight for women Men aren't the only ones who have an 'Ah-hah' here. Many women realize that the fear of being dismissed changes their behaviour too. Because women are on the defensive when they go into meetings, they unknowingly send a message to men to be careful. Then what happens? Men often react to that signal, without even thinking about it, by pulling back and becoming cautious – one of men's top challenges working with women. Women have to realize that men's behaviour is not intentional and that men are not deliberately dismissing them.

Challenge 2 – Women Feel Excluded

Women say:

- 'I always feel the real meeting takes place after the meeting, when the men go out for a drink.'

- 'I just don't seem to be able to get into the real corridors of power, no matter how hard I try.'

- 'Men use sports or war talk to describe strategies. I can't use that kind of language, so I feel I can't make my voice heard.'

It doesn't matter whether I'm talking to female lawyers, accountants, police officers or sales people. Most women in business have been in a similar scenario and have been left with more or less the same feeling. A woman comes to a table where men are gathered around, often talking about sport. She tries to fit into the conversation and even cracks a few jokes, but the men just take a look at her and carry on talking to each other. For the woman, it feels as though the men are deliberately ignoring her. Women already feel they have to struggle to be part of the team, and the cold shoulder treatment only confirms to them that no matter what they do, they will always be excluded just because they are women.

The famous 'meeting after the meeting' situation also serves to alienate female workers. In this situation, a group of men will go out for a beer after work. They don't invite their female colleague – maybe they assume she won't be interested, or maybe they don't even think of it. How does she feel? As if the real meetings take place after hours and she's shut out of them. So she feels she's deliberately shut out of decision-making.

If the woman is invited to attend the gathering, another dynamic sets in. When she arrives, the men are talking about football, or golf. Maybe she's interested, maybe she's not, but it doesn't matter. The men will be having fun, teasing one another, taking jabs at each other and carrying on with what's usually called male banter. Women feel this bonding going on between men. They don't want to be part of the locker-room talk, but they do feel excluded by it.

Women say that:

- They never know how to 'get on the inside'.

- They never 'get invited along with the blokes', or are actually told by their male colleagues, 'Believe me, you wouldn't want to come.'

- Their male colleagues 'congregate in a bloke's office, and sit around with other men, the boss included.' To women, it looks as if this just happens naturally, and they aren't included.

- Some male colleagues even attend men-only clubs like London's Garrick or Saville clubs, where women still can't be members. The message women hear is that men still feel comfortable excluding women.

Men's Reaction

Men's first reaction is usually, 'Well, I feel excluded too sometimes!' What men don't understand is that women feel they're being excluded because they're *women*. My male associate often takes this opportunity to jump into the discussion and explain women's point of view. He says:

'Men, take that feeling you've had of being left out of a decision once or twice and imagine it happening *every day of your working life*. Imagine you even see it coming when you walk into a boardroom meeting. Imagine it as a daily pattern. No matter how good you are, you're never invited to the important meetings! Lots of women feel this way, all the time.'

The insight for men Men usually understand, when another man explains it to them in those terms. Often a man from a visible minority will add, 'I can relate to that feeling.' Then men begin to understand that it's not about specific examples, but the recurring pattern: the water-torture drip. All women experience this, but men rarely do, because they're men.

Understand that this is a water-torture experience for women, and make sure that you introduce your female colleagues in a powerful and credible way in meetings with your clients, and that you acknowledge their skills and talents. This will eliminate this challenge.

The insight for women Again, when women hear men's reaction, they often start putting two and two together for themselves. The fear of being excluded, like the fear of being dismissed, often puts women on the defensive. A lot of times women aren't even aware of it. They get so used to feeling excluded that they forget it's happening! When they are reminded of this feeling in the workshop, they realize that it changes their behaviour. The fear of being excluded makes women act more aggressively, more brashly than they normally would.

Men pick up that signal. They don't necessarily understand it; they just react to it. How? By 'pulling back'; by being cautious and more careful. And that reaction, in turn, reinforces women's feeling that they are being excluded.

To solve this situation, women should be more vocal. Look for ways to collaborate. Be proactive. Invite yourself in. And men, remember: women *do* want to be invited in.

Challenge 3 – Women Feel Tested

Women say:

- 'With my clients, but even sometimes with my colleagues, it always feels as though there's this assumption that women just don't have what it takes.'

- 'I think women are scrutinized more than men – even by other women!'

- 'I feel I get questioned on my knowledge of technical aspects of my work a lot more than the men I work with do. People take it for granted that a man knows what he's talking about, but they wonder about a woman.'

Many women believe that they have to work harder than their male colleagues in order to prove themselves. 'I can only prove myself by sheer accomplishment, by being indisputably good,' they tell me. They constantly feel that their male colleagues are testing them, doubting their capabilities. They feel as though there's a different set of standards for women.

Women often feel they are assumed to be inferior. That feeling, in turn, undermines their self-confidence. It's as if everything – even the way they dress or the way they groom themselves – has the potential to lower their credibility. Some women say that they would never walk around in casual clothes on casual Fridays. They're afraid it would hurt their credibility. In fields where technical ability is an asset, many women feel that their peers and their clients constantly doubt their competency. The more traditionally male-dominated the field of work, the more women feel they have to meet higher standards than men do to get the same respect.

Women say that:

- 'Men get promoted for their potential, but women get promoted if they can demonstrate what they have already accomplished.'

- 'It feels as if there's an ongoing assumption that we have inferior skills or that we don't have as much technical ability as a man in the same position would.'

- 'There's an unspoken question, "Does she know her stuff?"'

- 'Men get credibility simply by doing their job, but women have to earn it. It's as if women have "a different starting point".'

Men's Reaction

When they hear women say this, a lot of men own up. Many men actually admit that they have more confidence dealing with other men, especially when it's a person they don't know. Men also admit that they feel in a real dilemma when they have *clients* who don't want to work with women. 'What do I do? Send them a woman and risk losing their business?' they ask. When they say this, they are usually defensive. They know that many women listening will blame them for not sticking up for women. 'You should stand up for her!' they say.

The men react by drawing on an argument that for most of them is a no-fail winner: money. 'If we bring in millions with this client, isn't it better just to play safe and send a man?'

This kind of reasoning is just salt in the women's wounds. This issue is particularly sensitive in companies and organizations where women don't have a strong presence: the police, the armed forces, traditional trades, even among litigation lawyers. Yet for men, the conversation triggers off their fear of being blamed. They have a hard time extracting themselves from the issue, enough to hear women's words for what they are: an authentic expression of how it feels to work with men. Fortunately, there are often men present who have gone out on a limb to promote women. 'When you push for women, it works,' they say.

The insight for men Because women tend to go to work with the feeling that they are being tested, they often feel they have to work harder, perform better and generally do more than their male colleagues to get the same recognition. Men notice this, but they jump to the wrong conclusions. They often tell me that women lack confidence and feel for some reason that they have to prove themselves. Well, it's not that women lack confidence. Women feel they are always being tested. They feel that they really do have something to prove.

And there's more. Women pick up men's feeling that they lack confidence. This makes them feel even more tested.

The insight for women Women can avoid setting off this self-perpetuating cycle of feeling tested by establishing their credibility right at the start. Don't wait for anyone to doubt you. You don't need to take on any inauthentic behaviour, like bullying or booming your voice. Introducing yourself in a straightforward manner, explaining who you are, what you do and what your background is, will do the trick.

Women need to be more assertive, to sell themselves more positively – have some training in this if necessary. Women should be more positive, practical and persuasive.

Challenge 4 – Women Find They Have Taken On Male Behaviour

Women say:

- 'If I want to be taken seriously, I have to be more forceful and more aggressive. I can't really afford to be myself.'

- 'I don't really like being so hard, so tough, and find myself directing people the way I do. The problem is, it works!'

- 'Sometimes I think my family would never recognize me if they saw me at work.'

When you've been in the workforce for, say, a decade, during which time you have felt ignored, dismissed and excluded, your behaviour does start to change. Many women say, 'You become more assertive and forceful and you even go as far as cracking sexist jokes.' But there's a price to pay for this behaviour. You may get respect, but neither women nor men will be comfortable working with you. You will also get nailed with the 'Dragon Lady' and 'tough broad' titles. Before you know it, you will have turned into a member of the Third Sex – a woman who acts like a man.

Most women who tell me about this phenomenon didn't know what was happening until it was too late. 'All I was trying to do was get respect,' they say. But because every aspect of their femininity seems like a drain on their credibility, many women slowly take on a new professional persona. It's a shock when they find out what happened. 'I scratched and clawed my way to the top. I worked on just being a straight, no-nonsense worker, and now I get called a barracuda,' one very senior woman told me.

Men's Reaction

When a woman takes on Third Sex behaviour, men simply stay as far away from her as possible. In order to understand why women do this, they usually need to hear it from another man. Here's how my male co-facilitator explains it to them: 'Imagine wearing a suit of armour to work every day. Imagine having to act as though you're someone else every working day, just to have the feeling that you're being taken seriously.'

Some of the women in the room admit that they've changed their behaviour so much and for so long that they're not sure they could give it up any more. Some of them don't think they would want to give it up. Why not? Because it works. It may make men uncomfortable, but it seems to work.

When they hear this, the light goes on for many men who can recall an incident when they heard their wife using a strange tone of voice on the phone with a colleague or client. It was her 'work' personality coming through.

The insight for men Men have to understand that women don't really choose to become the Third Sex. They feel they have no other choice. Women who end up turning into Dragon Ladies might do so for what they feel are good, justifiable reasons.

The insight for women The consequences of this choice are bad and women have to understand this. Maybe it seems to work, but in reality, Third Sex behaviour just leaves men more confused. They feel blamed, and act more carefully than ever. And of course, when men pull back and act carefully, that ends up making women feel as though they have to be Dragon Ladies in order to get respect. Women have to see the cost associated with this kind of behaviour – to themselves and everyone else. Trying to influence, rather than dominate people, is a much better way to earn respect.

Challenge 5 – Women Feel Like Tokens

Women say:

- 'Men always think I got this job because I'm a woman. It's so insulting and so humiliating to have to justify myself.'

- 'I didn't want affirmative-action policies. I just wanted the job I got!'

- 'I feel as if there is a price for getting this promotion. I'm under the microscope all the time!'

Many women tend to look at the workplace and see nothing but a no-win situation. When they do get employed, they feel that men are suspicious about how they got the job. Programmes to promote women add to this problem, as the perception is that a quota rather than qualifications is the determining factor in employing women. Women say: 'If I get the job or promotion, there is the sense out there that it's because I'm a woman, not necessarily because I deserve it.' The women who do succeed feel that they are under a magnifying glass. They feel that if they make mistakes, those errors will be attributed to their gender. They feel they are carrying the weight of the world on their shoulders.

Men's Reaction

When women talk about how it feels to be viewed as tokens, men usually react by saying, 'Yes, but we're victims of reverse discrimination so it all evens out.' Yet there's another, important aspect to this particular women's challenge. If men don't see it themselves, I encourage them in that direction and help them to make the connection to one of their own challenges. Men's reaction to the tokenism issue creates an even wider gap between men and women and makes it difficult for them to work together effectively.

The insight for men Although men react defensively at first, they eventually come to see that workplace policies to promote women do not mean life is a walk in the park for women everywhere. Those very policies add to women's feeling that they are being tested. Women's reaction to that feeling? They feel they have to work harder. They try to prove men wrong before they're even accused of anything.

Men will often say that the women they work with overcompensate or work too hard or are too perfectionist. Now they get a clue as to why women act that way. It's not because women are insecure. It's because they feel tested.

Men definitely have an 'Ah-hah' moment here.

The insight for women It's tough for women to feel good about their work when they fear they got their job because of equal opportunity policies. It's not an empowering feeling to carry around. And it ends up reinforcing their feeling of being tested and having to prove themselves. We've already seen what this does to women. The feeling of being a token makes women act defensively. It makes them feel they have to over-compensate. Sometimes it makes them more aggressive than they would normally be. They react to feeling like a token by working harder. But unfortunately, men often think this is a sign that women lack confidence.

My advice to women? Don't let yourselves fall into the trap of feeling tested. Develop a network of support around you. Don't try to bear the burden of proving women can do the job all alone.

Now you've had the golden opportunity to stand in the other sex's shoes for once. You've heard what the other sex has to say about working with you and you've seen how your own behaviour feeds those challenges.

Now you're ready to learn to do something to improve this situation. In the next three chapters, you'll see how men and women speak different languages, hear different stories and see different worlds. And you'll see what you can do to bridge the gap between the two different worlds men and women live in.

CHAPTER 6

Same Words, Different Language

Our conversational styles are different. If what you're after is not just self-expression but communication – then it's not enough for the language to be right; it must be understood.

Deborah Tannen, Professor of Linguistics, author,
You Just Don't Understand

So, men and women think differently. We process information differently. But we still speak the same language, don't we? Surely we can solve our problems just by talking. Actually, talking isn't the complete solution. Sometimes, talking is part of the problem. Men and women communicate differently. Even when we use the same words, we often don't mean the same thing. Most of us have an intuitive sense of this but we don't think about it much. We just bumble along assuming that the other sex means the same thing and interprets things the same way. We listen to the other sex from our own frame of reference. And we have already seen what types of misinterpretation that can lead to.

Without gender awareness, language is part of the problem. Men and women often don't mean the same things when they use the same words. They often don't hear the same words the same way. So what happens? When we communicate, we assume the other sex means the same thing as we do, and hears the same thing as we do. Then we evaluate their reactions from that standpoint. We read into what they say and do. We don't stop for a second to wonder if men, or women, might just be looking at things completely differently. Instead, we jump to conclusions. Or, worse, we miss the message entirely.

I learned a lesson very early in life about how people can think differently and what kinds of mistake I could make by assuming people thought the same way as I did. I left my native Denmark at a young age when I got married and moved to Italy. Very few cultures could be as different as those of Copenhagen and Rome. In Denmark, I had grown up in a world where people on the whole were calm, polite and reserved. Danes are very careful not to offend, to observe and not take too much 'air time'. They have a highly developed sense of what's appropriate and believe in good manners.

Imagine how I felt when I arrived in Rome with these ideas. When I suddenly found myself immersed in Latin culture, I thought:

- Why are the Italians so angry all the time?

- They're constantly fighting!

- They're so loud! Why can't they be quiet?

It's not hard to see my mistake. I was mapping Italian behaviour onto my Danish frame of reference. For the Danish, loudness signals anger, fighting signals a breakdown and noise is to be avoided. But not for Italians. What a mistake I was making! Slowly, as I got to know Italian culture better and mastered the language, my perspective changed and I started to see Italians from their own frame of reference. After about three months in Italy, I had to throw all my assumptions out of the window. I remember how my thinking changed. I realized:

- They're not angry. They're passionate!

- They're not arguing. They really love to talk and debate things.

- They're not interfering in other people's business. They're being open with each other. They ask about each other's problems because they care and bond that way.

I've often said that men and women would be better off if they actually didn't speak the same language. Maybe then we wouldn't take so many things for granted. We would pay more attention to how we say things and how the other sex interprets what we say. We would try to put ourselves in the other's shoes. We would try out ideas from another perspective. We would stop and think that maybe a certain word, or gesture or way of arguing doesn't mean the same thing for men as it does for women. We wouldn't take it for granted that the other understands our words and we'd make an extra effort to make sure they do.

Are men and women really so foreign to each other? The ones who attend my workshops certainly believe it after they've done the following 'communications' quiz. It includes a list of common, everyday words and phrases. I ask men and women to write down what they mean. You might want to try it yourself, before you read what men and women each say.

As you'll see, men and women have quite different ideas about the meanings of words that we all use every day. Imagine the confusion and frustration this creates. Not only do men and women understand the same words differently; they both jump to conclusions about what certain types of reaction mean, coming from the other gender. Luckily, there are solutions.

Before I tell you how differently men and women interpret the following eight words and phrases, please complete the quiz on the next few pages.

Language Quiz

If you are a man reading this, complete the section under **He**, and if you are a woman, complete the section under **She**. Now if you think that you might have the other gender figured out, I invite you to stand in its shoes and complete its sentences.

How Men and Women Listen

Yes!
HE What I mean when I use 'Yes!' is _____

_____

_____

SHE What I mean when I use 'Yes!' is _____

_____

_____

What do you think?

HE I'm being asked to _____

_____

_____

SHE I'm being asked to _____

_____

_____

What's the value of building a team?

HE I would build a team to _____

_____

_____

_____

SHE I would build a team to _____

_____

_____

How do you table an idea? _____

HE I would say _____

_____

_____

SHE I would say _____

_____

_____

How do you argue effectively?

HE My approach would be to _____

_____

_____

SHE My approach would be to _____

_____

_____

What is success at work?

HE I experience success at work when _____

_____

_____

SHE I experience success at work when _____

_____

_____

How do you listen effectively?

HE My approach would be to _____

_____

_____

SHE My approach would be to_____

_____

_____

The best way to convince is by:

HE My approach would be to _____

_____

_____

SHE My approach would be to_____

_____

_____

Now that you've answered this quiz, you'll get the opportunity to compare your answers with those of thousands of men and women. And when you see how differently men and women look at these statements, you'll see how those differences create misunderstandings, and learn how to prevent them.

'Yes'

What Men Mean
'I agree. That's final. Let's move on.'

What Women Mean
'I'm listening. I'm following. I'm open for discussing this.'

The Misunderstanding

For men, 'Yes' is the destination. When you've got there, there's nothing more to say. For women, 'Yes' means the trip has started. For women 'Yes' is not definitive. It means there is something going on. It's a word they associate with a *process*, not an *answer*.

Imagine the number of problems this simple but essential word can cause. Imagine what happens when men hear women say, 'Yes'; when they assume she means what he means, and then sees her react in a way that doesn't fit that picture. 'You never know when yes means yes with a woman,' men tell me.

Yet imagine how women feel when they hear men say, 'Yes'. They interpret it as an invitation to keep fleshing out a topic, and then find out that the case has been closed. This misunderstanding causes confusion, and leads to frustration and worse: it ends up reinforcing assumptions men and women already have about each other.

One man gave me the following example: 'I was on my way to a meeting and discussed my idea with a female colleague. She said, "Yes". But when we got to the meeting she turned around and started suggesting revisions.' He felt attacked and ambushed. 'I couldn't believe it! I thought I had her on my side! What on earth does "Yes" mean if it doesn't mean you agree?' he said. What do men conclude from such misunderstandings? That women are shifty, that you can never tell what a women means. And how do they react? By being careful. It's men's number one challenge working with women and that's why. It's a basic misunderstanding based on gender difference.

When a man abruptly closes a discussion with a 'Yes', and a woman thought it was just getting started, the woman feels dismissed. Women also sense this when men are being careful. 'Men are not really listening. Men are avoiding and dismissing us,' women say.

There is, of course, a cultural factor that exacerbates this whole situation. Women on the whole are brought up to be polite. One of the ways we're taught to be polite is to avoid saying 'No' outright. I remember a period in my days as a sales executive when I tried to unlearn that habit. Like many women, I have a tendency to avoid a flat 'No' by explaining my way around a negative reaction. But I felt that this behaviour was becoming a professional handicap. I sensed that people found me indecisive. So I practised saying 'No' without giving any explanation.

Of course it didn't work. I haven't changed. And why should I? It's futile for women to try to change their style. And it's futile for men to change theirs. So what should we do?

The Solution

The solution is to understand what the other means by 'Yes' and anticipate the misunderstandings that might come about. I suggest a simple technique I call 'Framing and Checking'.

For men Check what kind of 'Yes' you're getting. Is it 'Yes, that's final' or 'Yes, I'm following you, but let's explore this a little more'? Then tell women what kind of 'Yes' you need. If you tell a woman you need a final answer she won't feel she's being brushed off if you aren't open to more discussion.

For women Frame your 'Yes' with some more information so men know what kind of yes they're getting. Tell them, 'Yes. I'm listening,' or 'Yes. I see where you're coming from but I need to talk about it more.'

'What do you think?'

What Men Hear
Men hear the question as a call to action. They feel they are being challenged to take a position or make a statement or

deliver a decision. So when they answer, they try to deliver something definitive. They give their bottom line.

What Women Hear

Women hear the question as an invitation to talk about an issue, to express their thoughts and feelings about a topic or issue. For women, it's not a one-way street. When someone says, 'What do you think?' women hear 'Let's discuss this.' They try to initiate idea sharing. For women giving an opinion is often not as important as getting a discussion going. For them, the whole process counts. They will wait for the discussion to progress until it's the most effective time for them to express their feelings on the topic.

The Misunderstanding

The potential for misinterpretation here is great. When women react to the question by opening the discussion, men interpret this as 'She hasn't done her homework,' or 'She hasn't thought it through.' They think, 'Don't waste my time! Just give me the bottom line!' Men see women's indecisiveness as a sign that they lack confidence.

When men answer the question, 'What do you think?' with a definitive statement and then move on to the next issue, women feel they're being shut out. They think, 'I don't want a decision. I want to hear what you think.' They often feel men are being cold and distant when they give them categorical answers to questions, or that they are dismissing them. As one woman told me, 'It's as if men don't think I can make up my own mind about things. When I ask for an opinion they give me answers and solutions. But I'm not asking them to solve my problems for me!'

When women initiate idea sharing and ask for input, it's a way of being thorough. It makes them feel that they're doing their job well. Many women instinctively fear that in rushing to a conclusion, you may overlook things. Most men want to agree on solutions and implement them. They want to be spared the details because the details get in the way of them doing their job.

Many women also feel that building good relationships makes people work better. Asking for someone's opinion is sometimes as much a way to build rapport, as it is to get an answer. When men react in a way that makes women feel shut out, women are hurt and feel dismissed. They were, after all, extending an invitation to solidify a relationship.

The Solution

For men When women ask, 'What do you think?', check the question by asking 'Do you want exploration or do you want a definitive answer?' When men ask the question, it's wise to frame it. Ask, 'What's your considered opinion on this matter? Do you think this is good or bad?'

For women When women really want to know how men feel, they have to tell them specifically. They can preface the question, 'What do you think?' with a sentence like, 'I really want to hear how you feel about this,' or, 'I'm brainstorming. I really want us to take a good look at this problem and explore some possible solutions.'

'Teamwork'

What Men Hear
For men, teams are mainly a means to an end. The use of teams is to get the job done. If men think they can do a job on their own, they won't bother with a team.

What Women Hear
For women, teams are more than a means to an end. They are also an opportunity. To do what? To build relationships and long-term support bases for other projects. Women may not keep a specific team together after a job has been

completed, but they hope the relationships built among team members will continue.

The Misunderstanding

Since men see a team as the specific way to achieve a specific purpose, they tend to consider teams as temporary and finite. Since women see teamwork as an end in itself, they think of themselves as engaging in a long-term, ongoing process when they build teams.

The misunderstandings between men and women are predictable. Men tend to disband a team when the work is done and women want to use the team as the base for further collaboration. 'We had a winning formula,' women say. 'We had really started something. Why would we throw that away just because we finished the job?'

Men usually see building rapport as a frill. 'We're already pressed for time. Let's just get down to the task at hand,' they say. But women think the team will be more effective if there is good rapport between members. Without realizing it, men can make women feel as if all their valuable work is just being tossed out of the window, as though their work isn't appreciated, and they aren't valued.

The Solution

For both men and women Team building is one area where all businesses and organizations need to recognize women and men's distinct strengths and try to put both to use. Teams do work better when the members feel their common purpose, when they bond. The rapport that is created through a team can be a useful resource to be drawn on even after the team has achieved its immediate purpose. But, of course, for the team to achieve its goals there must be a sense of action and purpose.

Women need to appreciate the value of men's linear, goal-oriented approach, and men need to appreciate the value of women's skill in rapport building. Put these qualities together and you will have a winning team.

'Tabling an idea'

What Men Do
For men, tabling an idea means actually putting an idea on the table, clearly stating what the plan is. (In my opinion!)

What Women Do
For women, tabling an idea means putting an idea on the table, but the goal is to get suggestions and input, not to just state the plan. Women see it as a way to get a dialogue going.

The Misunderstanding

When they talk about feeling dismissed by men, many women mention this scenario: 'I state an idea. Everyone ignores me and then a man restates it and everyone loves it!' 'Tabling an idea' is the classic situation where this happens. Women think the objective is to get the dialogue going. They try to be inclusive of everyone's opinions and to encourage collaboration. But when they do this, men think women are uncertain, unprepared or unconvinced. They therefore reframe a woman's idea to clarify what was meant, to nail it down.

This situation leaves women feeling resentful and men feeling bewildered. As one man explained, 'One of my female colleagues didn't seem convinced of an idea she put forward at a meeting. I thought it was a great idea. I restated it to support her. And her reaction was that I stole her idea! I don't get it.' Women's inclusive style comes across to men as hesitancy. Men conclude that women lack confidence. When men state rather than suggest ideas, women feel that men aren't interested in their opinions and conclude that men are controlling.

The Solution

For men Men can also make it clear that they are open to others' input by saying, 'This is my idea. I think it's good, but it can always be better. I'm open to suggestions for improvement.'

For women Women can avoid feeling that their ideas have been stolen by using a simple strategy. They can say, 'I've thought this idea through. I'm clear on what I want to do but I want your input.' By stating their intentions this way, women 'frame' their ownership of an idea.

'Arguments'

What Men Hear
Men think arguments are debates confined to the single issue at hand. They don't have anything to do with what happened in the past.

What Women Hear
Women think arguments encompass a person's character across a spectrum of faults. Women see a pattern and that's what the argument is about. Women see signs of a person's character in what they say, and the arguments become about that, too.

The Misunderstanding

Women are acutely aware of patterns. A man will see a conflict stemming from specific circumstances, but a woman will immediately match that up to similar incidents, or even similar arguments from the past. If she saw certain character flaws as responsible for a past situation, she will see them at work in the present situation as well.

When women see a person acting a certain way, they tend to attribute this to his or her character. A man will say, 'He's behaving like an idiot.' A woman will say, 'He's an idiot.'

Women do this because of the way they collect memories. Remember from Chapter 3 how interconnected women's brains are? Women remember not only what happened, but also how they experienced an event. And they connect a past feeling to a similar one in the present very quickly. The men I talk to say they find women's 'linking' behaviour extremely frustrating. They think women are keeping score cards. Some men feel women are manipulating them when they do this. The truth of the matter is that for men to remember past experiences the way women do, they *would* have to keep score cards. Men hang onto the facts but they don't recall how an incident made them 'feel', the way women do.

The Solution

For men Understanding how women view arguments can help men to see the wider picture and perhaps avoid making hasty, and perhaps misguided, judgements about some situations.

For women Understanding men's view of 'arguments' can lead to a powerful insight for women. Men don't like to be part of the problem. They like to be part of the solution. When women expand an argument to talk about patterns they see, men get extremely frustrated. Women feel they are peeling away the layers of an argument to get to the real root of a problem, but men just feel they are getting further from a solution, not closer. If women are committed to resolving an argument, they should work on helping men to understand how apparently unconnected events do bear on the issue at hand, and do contribute to finding a solution.

'Success'

What Men Think Success Means
Winning.

What Women Think Success Means
Winning, *and* being valued by their colleagues and bosses.

The Misunderstanding

Women tell me that the number one reason why they leave their jobs is that they don't feel they're valued for their strengths. Men are perplexed when they hear women say this. What's being valued got to do with success, they wonder? For men, getting a bonus, a pay increase or a promotion, is enough to make them feel valued. Winning and being valued are the same thing. Succeeding according to the male version of success isn't enough for women.

It's easy for men to miss out on this one. 'If I don't say anything about her work, it means I value her,' they say. But women don't feel that they're at work *just* to produce results. Results alone aren't enough to give them satisfaction. Women often want their work to matter, and to feel this way, they have to hear it from someone.

The Solution

For men Understanding women's view of success can provide powerful insights for men. It doesn't take much effort for men to make women feel valued. Men just need to open their mouths and say what they think instead of taking it for granted that 'she understands'. Women need to hear that they are appreciated. And it's not because they are insecure. It's because for them, success means being valued by your colleagues.

For women Women need to realize that men don't understand how important being valued is to women. Make some allowances – ask for feedback. Men really may think your bonus was enough to make you feel valued.

'How to listen effectively'

What Men Do
For men, listening effectively means paying attention, quietly.

What Women Do
For women, listening effectively means nodding or vocalizing to demonstrate that you understand.

The Misunderstanding

Men often think women are agreeing when women are just showing that they're listening. My husband, a lawyer, tells me he used to fall into this trap during jury trials. While making his final remarks to the jury, he sometimes noticed that some of the women were nodding. He assumed he had them on his side. But during the opposing lawyer's summation, the same women kept nodding. 'It seemed to me that the same women were agreeing with opposite positions. I had no idea it was just their way of showing that they were listening.'

Men demonstrate their attentiveness by sitting still and watching. Even after seeing hundreds of groups of men in my workshops sit and stare at me while I speak, I still get the impression they're not listening, but they are. I call it the 'sports glare'. When women see men sitting stiff and staring while women talk, they conclude men aren't listening. Women's reaction? 'Men are dismissing us.'

Men consider it businesslike to listen attentively, giving full attention. Nodding and saying 'Uh-huh' seems like sucking up to them. When men watch women actively listening, they can't tell if the women are just listening, or agreeing. When women turn out not to be agreeing at all, it leaves men confused, frustrated and even feeling as though they are being manipulated. 'You can never tell what women mean,' they say.

The Solution

For men When listening to a woman speaker, it's useful to give the occasional nod or provide vocal feedback. 'I see what you're saying,' will do. It doesn't mean you agree or disagree. It just reassures the speaker that you're following her.

For women When women don't see any signs that men are actively listening, they often conclude men aren't listening at all. Some women managers have told me that after a presentation, they make men repeat what they said. Needless to say, this kind of patronizing behaviour probably doesn't help. Women should not assume that men aren't listening if they are sitting still. The best approach to is to check. I often ask men if they agree, or if they understand.

'The best way to convince is by . . .'

What Men Hear
For men, this means supporting your argument by facts, figures and careful logic.

What Women Hear
For women it means supporting your argument by personal experience and the experience of others.

The Misunderstanding

Several years ago, I was in an audience listening to the noted gender specialist Dr Helen Fisher talking about the results of some recent research on gender differences. To illustrate one point, she brought up the experience of some of her own friends. 'Just last night I heard some friends say,' she started. A group of men beside me reacted almost immediately. 'What the hell does what her friends say have to do with any of this?' they asked, shaking their heads.

Men think arguments should be supported by facts, figures and careful logic. Women often agree, but they frequently look to personal experience as well. For women, it's a way of being thorough. Women wonder how a solution to a problem might have repercussions in another area. They will weigh a particular decision or strategy against their own experiences, or others' experiences, as a means of exploring ways in which it might affect people when it's put into practice. When women bring personal experience into it, men think that's irrelevant. Men look for the facts. They react to women by saying, 'What's your personal experience got to do with this?' When men say this, women feel they are dismissing them and disregarding their strengths.

The Solution

For men Personal experience can be a valuable resource for understanding problems and coming up with solutions. I have met many male business leaders who have come to realize this and now actively seek out the input of their female colleagues, just to get their view.

For women Logic, facts and analysis are important too, particularly if you're trying to convince a man. Try to combine the two approaches to make a case. Ask the men around you for some input and ideas.

Take Responsibility

You might be wondering just where to start when you want to avoid misunderstandings caused by language. I often tell people, 'Take as much responsibility as you can when you listen.' If you recognize that gender differences create misunderstandings, it's up to you to do something about it.

The key is learning to listen actively.

When we talk, we want to be understood, but that tends to affect how we listen. While the other person is still finishing their sentence, we are already formulating a reply. We are busier thinking about what we have to say than making sure we understand what the other person is saying.

My advice? Listen actively. Change gears. Check to make sure you've understood the person you're listening to and make sure you're not listening through the filter of your own assumptions.

You don't need to memorize the misinterpretations in the quiz in this chapter. They are just examples of typical words and situations that men and women misunderstand when they listen to others 'reactively' instead of 'actively'. This chapter should be like a seed planted in your mind to remind you that when you're listening, you might not be hearing what you think you're hearing.

The next chapter will plant another seed in your mind. This seed is about perceptions. Perceptions are our own reality – but not everyone else's – and nowhere is the perceptual gap greater than between women and men. We go through life acting as if the other sex sees what we see. We rarely stop to wonder whether that's true. The unfortunate result, once again, is systematic misunderstandings between men and women. Yet once again, these can be overcome with some quite simple techniques.

CHAPTER 7

We See Different Worlds

Understanding means there's nothing to forgive.

Mother Theresa

If you ask a man and a women sitting in a room together whether it's the same room, they will probably think you're crazy. 'Of course it's the same room!' they will answer. But the truth is, it's not the same room. Even when they're looking at exactly the same thing, men and women see two different realities. Then they end up arguing over which room is real and which one is not!

Everyone knows what perceptions are. They are 'what we take in'. What people forget is that our perceptions are just percep-tions. They are not reality. How we see things depends on what we learned as children, or from our environment. I think of per-ceptions as filters because they shape and even block out other realities. Of course, men and women filter reality in very different ways. So it's almost as if we live in entirely different realities. And like the couple in the room, we end up arguing over who's per-ception is the real one.

A story from a real couple, Harry and Jane, shows how this happens. When Harry talks about their early courting days, he recounts all the problems he encountered trying to get to his first meeting with Jane's parents. 'I was late, then the car broke down,' he says. 'But I got there. And I won her!' Harry remembers their courting as a series of snapshot episodes that happened while he was trying to achieve his goal: winning Jane's hand in marriage. That's Harry's filter.

Jane doesn't talk about any of the details of Harry's journey to her parents' house. When Jane thinks of the couple's courting days, she remembers what happened when Harry got to her parent's house. She remembers who sat where at the dinner table, how her parents reacted and the look on Harry's face when he got there. 'I remember that your shirt collar was dirty. And you ate like a slob. It was amazing that my parents let me marry you!' she says. That's Jane's perceptual filter.

Harry doesn't remember any of these things. But Jane thinks these are the most important details. She has no idea why Harry even remembers what happened to him on his way to meet her parents. For her, it's beside the point.

There's nothing surprising about the fact that Harry and Jane have different versions of their courtship story. Men typically remember events in a very factual manner. For example, Harry remembers the exact time he left to go to Jane's parents' house and how long it took to get there. Men also tend to think in terms of achieving specific goals. All of Harry's attention was focused on what he had to do in order to get to his destination and win Jane's hand. It was a challenge to get there and the car broke down. That's what he remembers.

Women, on the other hand, remember things in an inter-connected way. They tend to focus on relational aspects of situations. Jane remembers how the whole process of Harry and her parents getting to know each other unfolded, and the finer details of everyone's interactions with one another. She recalls the expression on her parents' face when they saw Harry.

Harry and Jane joke about how they have such different recollections of the same event. They know they each have a different story, but they don't know why. After forty years of marriage, neither understands how differently the other looks at life. Instead, Jane thinks Harry doesn't pay attention to things. 'Why do you remember that the car broke down at 6.10 p.m. but you don't remember what you felt like when you met my parents?' she asks him. Harry is mystified as to why Jane remembers the things she does, like small things her mother said during the meal. 'What was so important about that?' he asks her. He thinks she is keeping some kind of score card.

Harry and Jane aren't alone. Men and women are equally mystified by how the other gender sees things. Unless you stop to consider how the other sex's different filters shape what they perceive, there's a good chance you will miss some essential information.

Men and Women's Sore Toes

We all have perceptual filters. We get them from our upbringing, our environment, our education and just plain old experience. Usually we don't even know we have them. But they come into play in all facets of our lives, shaping how we perceive what others say and do.

Perceptual filters aren't necessarily bad. They can be very useful. We all need to draw on past experience to make sense of what we see happening around us. We all need frames of reference. The problem is that filters sometimes prevent us from getting all the information we need. Unless we're aware of our filters, we may jump to conclusions about what we've observed, and risk making mistakes about other people's meanings and intentions.

Men and women are always surprised when I explain how perceptual filters affect their communications. We are so used to seeing things the way each of us does that we forget it's only our own perception. We assume that others perceive events exactly like we do. When they don't, we react. Typically, women think men deliberately ignore things. And typically, men think women read too much into things. It's a frustrating situation, but like Harry and Jane, we get used to it over the years and we just put up with it. We go into 'tolerance' mode. When events happen, we think we are reacting to the events. But really, what we are reacting to is our perceptual filters. Over our lifetime, accumulated perceptual filters get stronger and stronger, shaping our reactions, which, as you'll see, provoke other reactions.

Why do we put up with it? Men and women both have their own comfort zones. We fall into a certain kind of automatic behaviour. Women tend to love dealing with details: remembering birthdays, taking notes, organizing parties. Men tend to propose ideas and expect women to execute them. We don't walk around wondering why we think about things the way we do. If we did we wouldn't get any work done. Instead, we develop coping mechanisms to deal with friction. You say to yourself, 'That's just the way he (or she) is.' You brush it off and carry on.

But there's a danger in this automatic behaviour. As you'll see below, it causes some chronic misunderstandings between men and women. I call this 'stepping on the other sex's sore toes'.

Imagine you are walking on a beach. The water is sparkling blue and the sun is setting over the ocean and the breeze is gently swaying the trees. The problem is, you don't notice any of this because you have a sore toe and you've just stubbed it on a rock. It's been sore so long you forgot what you did to it in the first place. You've lived with it for years, so most of the time you don't notice it. But life being as it is, occasionally you'll stub it, or someone comes along and steps on it, and then you can't think of anything else. It just hurts!

Men and women are constantly stepping on each other's sore toes, without realizing it. It's certainly not that they want to or intend to, it's just that they're unaware that the sore toe exists.

Here are some of the typical misunderstandings I hear about over and over again. I'll show you how perceptual filters make women and men keep stepping on each other's sore toes, and tell you what you can do about it. The secret is learning to 'frame' what you say, offering your perspective of the situation and then 'checking' what the other sex says to make sure you've got the real message across. You can't get rid of perceptual filters, but you can avoid the misunderstandings they cause.

Men's Perceptual Filters

I've found that many women feel that their wrong buttons are being pushed by male behaviour in the workplace. Here are some of women's sore toes.

Women's Sore Toe – 'Protective Behaviour'

Women in my workshops often say, 'When I walk into a meeting, I can feel men's behaviour change instantly.' You have already heard about this in Chapter 4, where women talk about the challenges involved in working with men. When women have experienced this hundreds of times over their working lives, it wears on them. It confirms what women have come to believe: that men really do treat women differently.

One of the forms of this 'different' treatment is a kind of paternalism that some women also call 'protective behaviour'. Women in my workshops often say that men withold criticism or soft-pedal when discussing feedback with them. Women say men also make decisions for women based on the filter, 'I can't put a woman in a high-risk assignment or one that involves a lot of travelling.'

Other subtler behaviours from male colleagues also strike women as protective. Male colleagues will use bad language, then turn to the woman in the group and say sorry. As one woman told me, 'It's nice when they recognize that swearing is inappropriate, but singling me out and apologizing to me alone is not the solution.'

Men's Filter

Where does men's protective behaviour come from? I know from experience that men aren't deliberately over-protecting women. But men have been raised with the idea of taking care of women and it creates a perceptual filter that women need protection. Men do make an effort – even unconsciously – to act in ways they were taught are polite or caring.

They are also acting on an unconscious filter that says, 'Women need protection'. They usually don't even know it. It's not as if they have thought the situation through and come to the conclusion that women need help. It's more like a subtle orientation they were taught to have towards women. Most men act with the best of intentions. But for women in the business world, getting protective treatment can be a sore toe experience.

The solution for men Frame your intentions clearly. The first step towards improving communications with women is being direct with them. Say, 'I don't mean you to take this personally!' Men, you can be more direct with women than you think. For women, being direct translates as 'men care'. Women find it refreshing to discover that men are thinking about how their actions come across, and are willing to take a risk by revealing their concerns. Of course, when women feel that men are acting protectively, they should check men's intentions.

Women's Sore Toe – Feeling 'Excluded'

Being excluded from exclusive men's clubs is not what disturbs women the most. What kills women is the sore toe of casual exclusion that gets stepped on every day at work. This happens when men get together in each other's offices without inviting women, or when men never just drop in to women's offices the way they do in to men's offices. Women feel that sore toe when men don't include them in male groups and don't make any effort to get to know them. Women think, 'Men don't support us, men don't care about us and men don't value us as colleagues.'

Every week for years, Margaret, a stockbroker, had witnessed her colleague John invite two other male colleagues out to play sports such as squash, golf or hockey – without ever inviting her. As Margaret put it, 'What's depressing is that it gets so predictable.'

Men's Filter

What was going on? John wasn't deliberately excluding Margaret. He just acted as if he was excluding her because of a perceptual filter that told him, 'She's not one of the boys. I'm not sure what she is, but to be on the safe side, I'd better be careful.' For men, being with other men is simply a 'comfort zone'. Also, John didn't think Margaret would want to join in. 'I didn't ask because I didn't think it would be fun for her.' A lot of men tell me they feel this way. What they don't realize is that it's a filter. Women want to feel included. When men act on the filter that they don't, they step on women's sore toe.

The solution for men Don't make any assumptions, and if you can't help it, check out your assumptions before you believe they in fact exist. Men shouldn't stop playing golf altogether, but they should learn to use a little more imagination in the types of social activity they plan with colleagues. Open up the channels of communication, find a middle ground. Men and women do have specific preferences when it comes to leisure activities, but there are plenty they share too, like eating or wine tasting, or even going to a health club.

If you are creative, you can come up with plenty of win-win solutions. I have seen many companies change their social activities, or add some new ones. And men should take note: many women *do* like sports! So don't shy away from asking!

Women's Sore Toe – 'Sexist or Traditional Language'

When women and men hear the title chairman or president, they both tend to assume it's a 'he'. Yet for the rare woman chairman, it's hard not to take this kind of oversight personally. Traditional language structures feel exclusive to women. Sports analogies also hit many women's sore toe. I still don't know what an end-round discussion is. Some men will talk about a level playing field, batting average and losing a wicket. I don't know what these expressions really mean and lots of other women don't know either – or care! Military analogies are also common in the business world. But expressions like 'the war for talent', 'martial the troops' and 'marching orders' can be alienating for women.

Men's Filter

Women have to understand that men aren't deliberately trying to shut women out when they use this language. Men just have a filter from the past which says that sport and war are effective ways to make everyone understand a point. Not for women! Once upon a time, when the business world was populated almost exclusively by men, it made sense to use sports and military analogies. But that's not true any more and traditional language only feeds women's feeling of being excluded. The bottom line is: it's not a very effective way to communicate any more.

The solution for men It's easy: men should just use inclusive language. Instead of saying 'Good evening ladies and gentlemen,' say, 'Good evening everyone.' Everyone will feel welcome. I tell men: 'Don't think of it as "who's right and who's wrong". Recognize that it could harm your personal reputation. Men who use traditional language lose half their audience. Do your homework; language continues to evolve, and you need to evolve with it.'

Women's Sore Toe – Being Discounted or Discredited

It may be a new millennium, but many people still work from the assumption that women generally have fewer skills and less experience than men do. It's ingrained in most people's minds, both men and women. But for the women who are on the receiving end of this behaviour, it's another sore-toe experience.

I felt this a lot when I was working in sales. Men would over-explain things to me or paraphrase other men's points so I would be sure to understand. They probably weren't even doing this consciously. Yet it was humiliating. Women tell me they frequently feel they're being asked for more data or arguments than are necessary, as if men can take it for granted they don't know what they're talking about. At meetings, male colleagues repeat points to their female colleagues – in front of everyone. They seem to assume the women couldn't have understood.

Men's Filter

Men aren't aware that they're making women feel discredited. This behaviour is most frequent in fields where women don't have a strong historical presence, like law, finance, the high-ranking civil service, the armed forces or the police. In traditional male domains, men have a filter that women 'aren't in the right field'. The women who have succeeded in those fields frequently share that filter.

One woman I spoke to, a retired government official, admitted that she had refused to employ women for many years. 'I didn't think many women could handle the work, and I was afraid that if I had too many women working in my office, people would think my work wasn't that important, that it was women's work,' she said. She later realized the mistake she had made.

The solution for men Check if you've stepped on your female colleague's sore toe. If you realize you have, tell her it wasn't your intention and ask her to help you avoid making her feel discredited in the future. She will be happy that you care enough to try to avoid hurting her feelings.

Women's Sore Toe – Male Bonding

For most men, working with other men is a comfort zone. Women notice this and it may make them feel shut out. Women say to me, 'Even if two men don't know each other at all, they seem to instantly identify with each other. It's weird.' Men often discuss sport a great deal in their informal conversation, which as you've seen, makes their female peers feel excluded. When women talk to me about this, they refer to it as 'male bonding'. It's definitely a sore toe for women.

Men's Filter

Women see male bonding as a deliberate act of exclusion. But men don't intend their behaviour to send that message. Men tell us it really boils down to 'comfort zones'. Given the confusion about the rules, it's difficult for men to have a casual conversation with women at work. It seems to men to be much safer, and easier, to talk to other men, and sports are usually topics of common interest.

The solution for men Find topics of common interest. Get clear on ground rules on subjects that are inclusive. You can do this by asking your female colleagues what they're comfortable talking about. It doesn't mean that you should avoid talking about your favourite topics altogether. Remember some women love to talk about sport, some don't, in the same way as some men have other interests. It's just makes sense to check if a topic is of interest to everyone in the group.

Women's Sore Toe – When Men are Overly Cautious

When men act too formally towards their female colleagues, it comes across to women as being distant. Men can develop a strong sense of collegiality with other men but remain polite and courteous with women. When this politeness never gives way to professional familiarity women feel slighted. Women conclude, 'he's insensitive or cold, or he doesn't care about me' and imagine 'he doesn't take me seriously'. It adds to women's feeling of being excluded or dismissed.

Men's Filter

Men's formal behaviour doesn't come from indifference towards women. They mean it as a form of respect, and a way to avoid being misinterpreted by women. Men would much rather err on the side of formality, rather than be blamed for being too familiar with their female colleagues. Men are genuinely afraid of offending women.

The solution for men You probably guessed what I'm going to say. Don't hide behind your comfort zone. Make sure you keep the communication channels open, and you will no longer be concerned about offending, because you will know what works.

Women's Perceptual Filters

As I said in Chapter 4, it's hard to get men talking about the challenges they face when working with women. Typically, men don't spend as much time thinking about relationships with their colleagues as women do. 'We go to work to do a job,' they say. But this doesn't mean that men don't feel challenges working with women. Asking the question the right way is the key to getting men to talk. For instance, they don't think about whether women make them feel disempowered but they will talk about what makes them pull back.

Women certainly do step on men's sore toes. And they do so because of perceptual filters that make them look at the world a certain way.

Below you will see the behaviour that makes men pull back. Women, watch how your behaviour sometimes comes across to men. Understanding your own perceptual filters is the first step to avoiding the misunderstandings they lead to.

Men's Sore Toe – 'When Women Don't Articulate Problems Clearly'

Men in my workshops say, 'Women throw one conversation into another,' or 'When women discuss a problem they drag all sorts of other problems into it.' It's true. When women tackle problems they look for solutions by expanding the problem into other issues. Men find this frustrating. To them, it sounds as though women are just adding new problems to the pot, obscuring the issue at hand and getting further from a solution. 'When I present a problem, women come up with a whole series of other problems. I don't know which problem we're focusing on here,' men say. Some men conclude that women just aren't focused, that they're not very good problem-solvers. Others say that women are vague or chaotic, or that they meander. Some men even think women are deliberately trying to confuse them.

Women's Filter

Women are not vague or chaotic or less focused than men. Women just automatically see issues in terms of how one problem is linked to another. Women use talking to focus. Men focus first, then talk. It's not a better or worse way to see problems. It's just different. For a man, the problem is a single one. He wants clarity on it, before anything. Women don't stop to think that men hear the word 'problem'; men don't really hear the same thing as women.

The solution for women Frame your conversation first. Before you even open your mouth, think about what it is you need from him in this conversation. If you are looking to explore a problem before even trying to solve it, you'll have to say so. Men assume you want a solution, end of story!

Men's Sore Toe – 'Women Generalize'

Men say, 'Women are always taking one situation and expanding it to generalize about a whole lot of things.' What men call generalizing is really seeing patterns. Women tend to remember the patterns in things and use that information to analyze present circumstances. Men find this frustrating because it comes across to them as blame, as 'dragging things back from the past'. They say, 'A woman takes one situation and then makes it sound as if I'm always like that.' A male colleague is late and the female colleague reacts by saying, 'You're always late.' Perhaps he is often late, but to him it feels like a sophisticated form of blame.

Women's Filter

When women generalize, they aren't setting out to blame. They are just behaving naturally. Women tend to look at events and see patterns. Women remember similar behaviours from past situations and they match them up. And when they see a pattern, they do tend to attribute it to someone's character. They can't help it (and sometimes they're right). The problem is that they forget that men don't see the world the way they do. A woman will think she's making an observation, but a man will hear her generalizing, 'score-keeping', and blaming him. When women can't name the patterns they see, they feel frustrated.

The solution for women Drop the words 'always' and 'never' from your vocabulary. I know it's hard because you can easily see the pattern in situations. But these two words only invite men to argue about the actual frequency of an incident. In your discussions with men, keep things isolated and specific to the point at hand as much as possible. Men tend not to see the patterns; they want to stay focused on one issue, sort it out and move on.

Men's Sore Toe – 'Women get Emotional'

Men say, 'Sometimes I just want to tell women to get over it! The kinds of thing that make them upset would just go over the top of my head!' In fact, women are not more sensitive than men. They just process information differently. We are taught to internalize things. Women tend to think first of how they may have affected an event or situation. They wonder, 'What did I do to cause that?' They internalize conflict, reacting perhaps with tears, while men externalize conflict and explode. Men interpret women's reaction as demonstrating lack of confidence or weakness. They say women can't take it like a man. 'There's no crying allowed in rugby!' Well, women don't react like men. Women aren't men.

Women's Filter

Women don't cry to gain sympathy or to draw attention to themselves. Internalizing conflict, for women, is like breathing. It just happens. Men externalize and are more likely to explode. There's no hidden agenda in women's way of reacting to conflict. Once men understand this, it becomes a tremendously useful insight in their dealings with women and much of the uncertainty and apprehension in dealing with their female colleagues falls away.

The fact that tears in the workplace, for women, are almost always an expression of frustration and anger, just as thumping a desk might be for a man, is a real 'Ah-hah' for most men. They can now replace the filter 'Women are sensitive' with 'Women feel stress and conflict differently, and express anxiety differently from men.'

The solution for men Relax! Crying does not mean women are falling apart. Most of the time there's nothing for you to do but listen while women express their frustration. Pass the tissue, and let women clear the air and vent their frustrations. Remember: the worst thing you can do is to say to a woman, 'Don't cry,' or 'Don't get so emotional about this.'

Men's Sore Toe – 'Why Don't Women Correct Inappropriate Behaviour?'

Men say, 'I wish women would just tell me what's the matter. Instead, they walk off in a huff, and then bring it up days later!' It's true. Women do often hesitate before telling men they're unhappy about certain behaviour. Why? Most women are afraid that when they confront men about their behaviour, they'll be brushed off and interpreted as being overly sensitive.

Women's Filter

There are reasons why women don't confront men immediately about inappropriate behaviour. Women are acting on the filter, 'Men dismiss us.' Women don't want to appear petty for addressing one incident, but will make a mental note and observe if it happens again, then address it; or they will wait until a later time to bring it up, when they feel it may be more appropriate or they're on safer ground. This way, women will fear being given the brush-off less because their case is stronger.

The solution for women Telling men (in private) straightaway is the best policy. Keep remembering that, for the most part, men's actions aren't intended as personal slights. It's a challenge to be straightforward about your reactions, but doing so will free you from the burden of constantly mulling things over in your head. If you get stuck, use the methods in Chapter 10.

Men's Sore Toe – 'Women Don't Get to the Point'

Men complain that women fail to understand their need to get to the bottom line. 'Women talk around the point without seeming to move towards a solution,' they say. It's an especially sensitive issue in their personal lives. A man will be driving with his wife to a restaurant and she will say, 'Remember that great Chinese restaurant we went to last year? It's just around the corner.' His reaction? 'Yes, I remember.' And he keeps driving to the original destination. When his wife is hurt that he didn't get the message, he's perplexed and frustrated and feels as though he's being blamed for something without knowing exactly what he did wrong.

Women's Filter

At work, this translates into a classic misunderstanding between men and women. Men say a woman will beat around the bush and then, 'blame me because I couldn't read her mind.' What they don't understand is that women are acting on a filter. What seems to men like an obscure reference shows up to a woman as a 'direct hit'. Women don't understand why men don't see that a passing remark about the restaurant is really a suggestion to actually go there. Men just think it's a historical observation and don't take it any further.

The solution for women When you communicate with men, be more direct. Don't be pushy, but use clear, 'action' oriented language. Frame your conversation 'I have a request. I would love you to do this for me.' Men will be happy to hear requests framed in this way.

Take Ownership of Your Filters

Do we own our perceptual filters or do they own us? Many people have difficulty imagining that filters are just part of who they are. At the beginning of one of my workshops, David, a particularly brash manager, insisted he didn't have any filters. 'You can't change the way I am,' he said. 'I'm a control freak and that's that.'

David certainly acted like a control freak. I remember watching his colleagues shudder as he summarily silenced them in mid-sentence. When his colleagues spoke he would hold up his hand like a football referee and tell them to 'hold that thought' (of course, they always forgot it before he gave them a chance to speak). When they tried to explain their points of view he interrupted them.

The answer to the question is: filters own us until we become aware of them, recognize them and take ownership of them.

David realized he had a filter that said, 'You have to act "controlling" to be in control.' That filter came from a specific experience early in his career when his partners abandoned him. 'I made a decision at that point that it was better to control everything myself than to be left high and dry, and I've held on to that philosophy ever since.'

David recognized his filter. He could see that his behaviour wasn't really 'him' at all. He realized that it was actually counterproductive. Things did get done, but he left a wake of frustrated and discouraged colleagues behind him. More important, he understood that his controlling behaviour was actually defeating his real commitment to help his team accomplish its goals.

So he took responsibility for his filter. He decided to change his behaviour. It really was that simple. Once he had 'the eyes to see' his filters, he was able to change his behaviour and work towards his real goal.

David's story ended well, but it could easily have led to a disaster at his company. David's perceptual filter had created a blind spot. He simply didn't see how his actions were perceived by his colleagues. In the next chapter, you'll hear how men and women's perceptual filters create typical blind spots, which lead to huge misunderstandings. And you'll see what you can do to avoid being a victim of your blind spots.

CHAPTER 8

We Hear Different Stories

To discover the truth in anything that is alien, first dispense with the indispensable in your own vision.

Leonard Cohen, author and poet

In the water most of us swim in at work, there are an awful lot of stereotypes floating around: 'Men don't listen', 'Women talk too much', 'Men like hard jobs', 'Women like background work – their career isn't their first priority' and 'Men are the primary income earners.' Stereotypes can be blatant or subtle. They are almost always myths. Yet the real problem is not really the ideas themselves. The real problem is what we do with them. We act on stereotypical assumptions without checking to see if they are true. They are usually not true.

And this creates 'blind spots'. Blind spots are things we literally don't see, information we don't get from the other sex because of assumptions we've made about how they will react or what they will think in certain situations. They are a major cause of misunderstanding between the sexes.

Maya's story

The following story shows a typical case of how a blind spot almost ruined a working relationship and almost pushed a valuable employee out of a company. You may recognize yourself in one of the central characters.

Maya, an engineer, mother of three, and one of the top technical experts in a large computer firm, had decided to leave her job. When I met her she was already considering an offer from a rival firm. It was a familiar story. After years of working hard with stunning results, she felt her bosses still didn't appreciate her work. She decided enough was enough.

Maya enjoyed her job and got on well with her colleagues, so I probed her to find out in more detail why she had decided to leave. It turned out her company had decided to open a new division in Australia and, although it would not be promotion, Maya had felt she was the ideal candidate for the position of project manager in this large, high-profile venture, which would require a three-month stay abroad. However, the job had not been offered to her, and she had only heard about it after someone else, less qualified than she was, was being considered for the position. No one had asked her if she was interested. Maya was so humiliated and offended by this that she decided not to even bring it up with her boss. As far as she was concerned, it was proof he didn't respect her or recognize her qualifications. 'It's clear what he thinks of me. It's because I'm a woman.'

I suspected Maya was suffering from a blind spot and asked her if she was willing to test her assumptions and ask her boss why he hadn't considered her for the Australia job. It was not an easy step for her, since she had already made up her mind to leave, but she decided to give it a go. 'Leave your assumptions at the door. They may be right, but forget them for a minute,' I told her. Instead of telling him she was hurt, which would put him on the defensive,

I told her to 'frame' her comments. So this is what she said:

'Tom, I have assumed that you didn't even consider me for the position in Australia. I want to check that assumption.'

Tom was floored. 'I just assumed that a woman like you with three small children wouldn't want to up sticks in the middle of the school year and move to Australia for three months,' he said. 'I didn't want to put you on the spot and make you decline.'

Tom was in many ways a typical sales manager. He was an 'action' man – committed, aggressive and result-oriented. He was used to living by the rules of a reactive environment where there wasn't much time to sit back and reflect on things. But he was also a fair man who tried to look out for his colleague's best interests. He knew Maya was perfect for the job, and he had agonized over whether to ask her or not. But in the end, he had thought it would hurt her to offer her the job.

Maya was stunned and angry, but she could see that Tom meant well. Most importantly, she could see that the situation was salvageable. 'This job in Australia would be the best thing that could happen to me!' she told him. 'I have been waiting for an opportunity like this to come up for years!'

Where was the Blind Spot?

Maya and Tom both had blind spots. They both had preconceptions about what the other thought based on stereotypical ideas they had about the other sex. Tom had assumed Maya put family first. He had decided not to offer the job to Maya because he had thought that she wouldn't want to disrupt her family life with a move to Australia. Maya had assumed that Tom didn't respect women. Because of that assumption, she concluded that she had been unfairly and unreasonably discriminated against because of her gender.

Luckily, they recognized their blind spots before it was too late. Tom offered Maya the job in Australia. Maya got special permission for her children to miss some school and they and her husband flew over to join her for a month. When she got back, she said it had been one of the most challenging and exciting projects she had ever worked on.

Blind Spots at Home

Blind spots can be costly for everyone, and not just at work. Several years ago a young executive named Victoria came to me for advice about a marriage breakdown. Victoria had been on a retreat to 'think and refocus herself'. On returning, she had decided to get a divorce. 'The relationship has changed. All Tim wants to do is spend time apart, each of us doing our own thing.'

Victoria assumed Tim was losing his commitment to the marriage and losing interest in her. Like many people, she sought relief from questioning her relationship by actively seeking a resolution. She went off on a retreat and came back with a decision. She drew a circle around the meaning of Tim's actions, sealed that box shut, and moved on to action – which in this case, meant getting a divorce.

It turned out that Victoria had a blind spot. Like Maya, she had assumed men don't care. I encouraged her to tell Tim about her assumptions before she announced that she wanted a divorce. When she did, Tim couldn't believe his ears. He said he was as committed to the marriage as ever. And there was a good explanation for his actions. Tim felt strongly that couples needed to be independent.

As his relationship with Victoria grew, Tim worried they were getting 'too fused'. He reacted by scheduling more outings with his mates and by encouraging her to do more with her friends too. He just assumed Victoria thought like he did and would automatically understand. Luckily, Victoria and Tim realized they had made wrong assumptions about each other before it was too late.

Blind Spots are Self-perpetuating

Men and women everywhere tend to make the same assumptions about each other and often end up with the same blind spots. Then they take the same actions based on those blind spots. The real tragedy is that those actions usually end up feeding the original assumptions.

Take women's assumption that men don't listen. Women often react to this assumption by actually talking more. Women tell me, 'Since men don't listen, I reckon I have to talk more, explain more, and repeat myself a lot. If I talk long enough he'll eventually catch on.' How do men react when women keep talking to them? To a lot of men it sounds like lecturing. So they switch off. At home, men roll their eyes and say, 'Yes dear.' At work, men say to themselves, 'Here we go again.'

Then what happens? Women think they have the proof of their original assumption, that men don't listen. What a mess our assumptions get us into.

Breaking the Cycle

How do we avoid becoming victims of self-perpetuating blind spots? The first thing to do is to question assumptions we are making. It's hard, but there is no way around it.

The clue is learning to listen. There are two ways of listening. Most of us just listen like a screening process. We listen for what we already know. We compare what we hear to what we already know and decide if it's 'right or wrong'. When you listen this way, all you are doing is validating your own opinions and assumptions. You're not really learning anything new.

What you need to do is to listen actively. Active listening means consciously interrupting your screening process so that you can really learn new things, or new ways of looking at the old things. You have to turn listening into an opportunity to learn, put aside your assumptions and opinions, and become open to new discoveries, some of which might well challenge those very assumptions and opinions you had previously held. Active listening lets you stand in the other person's shoes, to learn from, and about, their perspective. It lets you get inside the other person's head to see what they're trying to say. Active listening is what gives you those 'Ah-hah' moments.

How do you do that? Follow these guidelines:

1. 'Take ownership' of the situation. It's the only way to avoid becoming a victim of your own blind spots. Try to recognize your own blind spots before you judge and evaluate others. Ask yourself, 'Is there something in what this person is saying that I'm not understanding?' There probably is.

2. Ask questions. Ask the person you're listening to what they mean. What's their opinion on the issue? How does this appear to them?

3. Use checking and framing strategies. First check whether your assumption is true. Maybe it is, but there could be more to it than you think. Then frame your question in a way that avoids putting your boss or employee or colleague – or spouse – on the defensive.

4. Don't rationalize or screen their responses. Ask yourself whether you are having a true dialogue with the other person. If you're in a true dialogue, if you're really listening actively, it means you're learning something about the other person's perspective that you never thought of before.

5. Don't get on the defensive yourself. 'What you said hurt me,' is not a good way to get honest feedback. Take ownership of your assumptions with a phrase like, 'I made an assumption

about what you said to me. I just want to check and see if that's what you really meant.'

6. If you need to remind yourself about why it's so important to check your assumptions, ask yourself some simple questions: What is my long-term commitment here? Do I want to make this relationship work?

Over the years I have noticed that there are some assumptions men repeatedly make about women, and some assumptions women repeatedly make about men. All the assumptions create blind spots that lead to misunderstandings. The solutions are usually simpler than you think. Have a look at the following examples.

Men's Blind Spots

Here are some of the assumptions men make about women.

'You have to hold back with women'

What Men Assume

Men often assume they have to hold back with women because women are more sensitive than men are. The assumption usually comes from experience. Men may have seen women cry over difficult situations at work, and think they should avoid provoking women at all costs. Many men come to me asking for advice on how to talk to female employees. They know they have a communication problem. They are holding back, and they can tell it doesn't work, but they don't know what to do.

Rick, a senior manager at HSBC, was one of those men. He said, 'I'm harder on the men who work for me than I am on the women.

I march forward with the men, but I'm always soft-pedalling with the women. I mean, sometimes I really dress the men down. I'll even tease them about their tie or something. But God forbid I so much as comment on what women are wearing!' To his credit, Rick had already put two and two together. 'Women tell me they think I'm not listening. And the truth is, I pull back with women. I definitely treat the men and women in my company differently. I have to! Women take things so personally!'

Like many men, Rick assumed that women take things personally. I urged him to check that assumption.

Finding the Blind Spot

The truth is, women often do take things personally. As we saw in Chapter 3, because of the way women's brains work, they don't separate emotions from the rest of their brain processes in the same way that men do. But the fact that women react emotionally to situations doesn't mean they 'can't take it'.

That's what Rick found out, when he scheduled a meeting with the women on his executive committee to check his assumption. He told his female colleagues: 'I have had an insight recently that I make an assumption that women always take things personally. I realize that I soft-pedal with women to avoid that. Do you feel that I do this, and if so, how can I address issues differently with you?'

The women's reaction? 'It's true!' they all said. 'We do take things personally.' Then they delivered the really surprising news. 'What's the problem?' they asked Rick. 'We cry, then we get over it. As long as we know you're being straightforward with us, that's what really matters. What really hurts is when you beat around the bush with us.'

What Rick discovered by checking with his female employees was that he had a blind spot. With the best of intentions, he had assumed that the women wanted to be treated with kid gloves. He was completely wrong. What the women wanted was to be treated in the same way as the men.

'Women are more comfortable dealing with women'

What Men Assume

Men assume women are better equipped to deal with other women's problems, and prefer dealing with women. They probably get this idea from their upbringing and socialization. Women may even unwittingly feed this idea themselves, by setting up 'women's' committees for various activities. Wherever this assumption comes from, men act on it without checking it. In business, men often shift responsibility for dealing with women onto other women. Men ask women to get into groups to work on women's issues in a company, or they send a woman to take care of a personal problem with another woman. Lots of companies make the assumption that female clients also feel more comfortable dealing with women, whether it is in sales or services. Most companies act on this assumption without testing it.

A large retail store that sells men's clothing called me because it had the following problem. Years earlier, the store had reacted to a study which had revealed that most men's clothes were actually bought by women. 'All our salesmen are men,' they said, 'so we employed some women in sales.' The problem? The policy backfired. The saleswomen actually had a *harder* time selling to women. They even had the feeling that the women who came into the store were avoiding them.

I told the store's management that they might have a blind spot. I suggested that they conduct some focus groups with women, carefully framing their questions. Managers at the store assembled the focus groups and asked them: 'We have been making the assumption that women don't like to buy from men. Is it true?'

Finding the Blind Spot

Well, the assumption was partially true. The women said they didn't like buying from men. But the company had a blind spot. The women said they were uncomfortable buying men's clothes simply because the salesmen didn't know how to treat them. They repeatedly said that they didn't necessarily want to be served by women. 'We just want to be taken seriously by male salespeople,' they said. The women said that if the men knew how to treat them, they preferred salesmen to saleswomen, since they wanted a man's input on their purchases. 'Train your salesmen how to treat women shoppers,' the women said.

Many companies resist seeing this kind of blind spot for a long time. Why? Companies often make large investments based on wrong assumptions, so they aren't too open to seeing their blind spots. This company had employed female sales staff thinking this would solve the problem and now it didn't want to start again with a different solution.

Do women really prefer dealing with women and women's issues? No. Professional women don't want to be stuck in women's ghettos, no matter what kind of company they work for.

'Women don't want tough work, or tough clients'

What Men Assume

Men tend to make two assumptions about tough clients: that those clients will prefer dealing with men, and that women won't want to deal with them anyway. This also, almost certainly, comes from men's socialization. Small boys are taught not to hit little girls, so they grow up thinking women can't throw a decent punch, and wouldn't want to anyway. This attitude is particularly prevalent in non-traditional fields, like the police. I saw it in action in a workshop with the Los Angeles Police Department, where women were systematically relegated to lower risk positions like traffic and clerical work.

The 'tough client' scenario is even more prevalent. Bob, a manager at an international consulting firm, told me he avoided sending women out to work with some of his clients. 'I've got this male client from the Middle East,' he told me. 'I could never send a woman to work with him, for his sake and for hers. He would resist working with a woman and she would pay the price for it.' Bob repeated that he wasn't passing any kind of judgment either on his client or on his female colleague. It was just a situation he assumed it was best to avoid, he said, for practical reasons. The problem was that he had a female colleague, Mary, who was perfectly qualified, and well suited to work for this particular client, having been a team member working on an earlier project for him.

Finding the Blind Spot

Bob had two blind spots, one with his client and one with Mary. I pointed out to Bob that he was acting on two assumptions and I pushed him to test them. 'Could you be making assumptions about your client and Mary that could both be wrong?' I asked him. Bob said he was positive the client didn't respect women. So I asked him, 'What makes you so sure he'll react to Mary the same way he reacted to his secretary?'

Bob said he was willing to test his assumptions. He checked with Mary. 'I'm assuming you wouldn't want to work with this client. Am I right?' he asked.

Mary's answer surprised him. 'I'd love to work for this client,' she said. 'I know his file and his business inside out. I know what he needs. It would be a great challenge.' And she added, 'I also know from experience that he doesn't treat all women like he treats his secretary.'

Then Bob decided to test the assumptions he had made about

the client's preference for men. He told the client, 'I think I've got the best person for the position of team leader on your project,' he said. 'I've hesitated because the candidate is a woman and I know the project will involve you being together a lot. I have assumed you wouldn't be comfortable with that.' And then Bob told him it was Mary.

The client's answer? 'Oh, Mary,' he said. 'I remember her. I'd love to meet her again.' The client revealed that he thought she had done outstanding work in the past, from what he had seen, and he loved her style. So Bob decided to give Mary the job, after all.

Assuming women don't want to take risks creates a big blind spot for men. Women love challenges as much as men do. Those who are courageous enough to enter non-traditional fields are certainly risk takers to begin with. They can deal with tough clients as men can, when it's necessary – and they can often 'read' clients so well that they can find ways around potentially very tricky problems.

Women's Blind Spots

Men aren't the only ones who make stereotypical judgments about the opposite sex. Women's assumptions about men also create blind spots.

'Men like the status quo'

What Women Assume

Lots of women – particular those in the denial stage of gender awareness – think men don't want anything to change. They believe men are more than happy with the 'traditional business model' and the traditional work environment. Or they believe that deep down, most men would rather go back to the good old days, before they had to work with women.

Christine, a human resources manager at an investment bank, made this assumption. She had been trying to address gender issues at work for years, but said she couldn't even get the conversation started. Her explanation? 'Men just want to keep things the way they are. As far as I'm concerned, if I want things to change, I'll have to leave and try somewhere else.'

Christine felt that she knew this for a fact, but in reality, she had made some assumptions based on what she had observed. There had been several cases of harassment at her bank and she had the mandate to address the issue with fifteen senior executives, all men. Whenever she tried to get things like harassment or equal opportunities on the agenda at meetings, she felt resistance from them. 'Men don't bring up gender issues on their own,' she explained. 'It's never on the agenda.' She had overheard some male colleagues joke about 'the good old days'. 'I give up!' she told me.

Finding the Blind Spot

Christine had a blind spot. There may be one in a thousand men in the working world these days who truly wish for the return of the good old days. Every human resources survey shows this: men want change too, especially – but not only – younger men. A recent Du Pont study showed that 62 per cent of men surveyed would choose quality of life over more money or promotion, if they had the choice.[1]

So I challenged Christine to test her assumption. 'Is it possible that you are making assumptions about your colleagues based on your own filter that "men don't care"?' I asked. It took her a year to decide to check her assumptions, but she eventually did and then she saw her blind spot. 'I have the assumption that you don't want anything to change,' she announced at a meeting with the fifteen executives. 'All we talk about is keeping shareholders happy, net profits and growth. We never talk about the workplace environment. Is it true that no one here cares about our workplace environment?'

The answer was a resounding 'No.' Fourteen of the fifteen executives said they really wanted change. They thought the environment at the bank was hostile and there were too many 'power plays', too much condescending behaviour and too many put-downs between colleagues.

'So,' Christine asked, 'Why have we never talked about these things at meetings?' Their answer really took her unawares. 'It was never on the agenda,' they said. At meetings, the executives felt pushed to address exactly what was on the agenda and get through it. They were aware there were problems in the workplace environment. Many had read about harassment and had thought about it. Many expressed the desire for a more inclusive and diverse work environment. Several feared the bank was getting a reputation for having a harassing environment and wanted to do something about it, but didn't know what to do. Their tendency to be goal-oriented and focus on business priorities made them stick to the agenda in meetings.

Christine had a blind spot. She thought men didn't care when actually they were just acting in a normal, natural male work style: they followed the agenda in a logical way. When she put 'workplace environment' on the agenda, the executives were happy to collaborate on research, and to address problems in the working environment.

'Men are Insensitive'

What Women Assume

Woman constantly see situations at work where men don't react in the way they think they should have. Someone will criticize a woman at a meeting and she will say of a male co-worker after-wards, 'He should have stood up for me.' What do women con-clude when men act this way? That men are 'insensitive'. Women complain that men don't notice their reactions. After experiencing a difficult situation at work, women say the men around them just carry on as if nothing is happening.

Peggy, a nurse, fell into this trap with Leo, a surgeon she worked with. For ten years, Peggy watched him visit patients in their rooms and give them the facts about their operation or condition. His business-like, detached approach looked like a lack of empathy to Peggy. As a nurse, she felt that all she did was to clean up the emotional mess he left behind after his patient visits.

Finding the Blind Spot

One day, Leo had to operate on a 16-year-old girl who was victim of a gunshot wound. After the operation, Leo dissolved in tears, right in the operating room. Peggy could see that Leo did have feelings after all. When she asked him why he had never expressed any emotion about his patients before, he told her he had, but only in private, never at work. Actually, he explained to her, he got rid of most of his frustration on his daily 10-kilometre run. 'That's when I let it all out,' he said.

Most men are more sensitive than they appear to be to the women they work with. It's a big blind spot for women who inter-pret men's 'detachment' as lack of feeling or insensitivity. Leo was sensitive. He just didn't express it the way Peggy expected him to, and she assumed that he didn't have any feelings at all. The trap she fell into was assuming that Leo was cold and heartless, when really he just showed a classic male tendency – emotional containment. You respect the patient by not laying bare your own feelings.

What's going on? Men have emotions, but they deal with

them differently than women do. Even as little boys, men are taught to suppress their emotions by not showing them. Later, in the traditional work environment, they are taught to depersonalize things, and to deal with problems in a detached, rational way. In other words, all their lives men are told to take charge of their emotions. So that's what they do. Women need to understand men's way of dealing with emotions before they jump to conclusions about men not caring.

'Men Think They Can Do Things Better'

What Women Assume

Women who work in teams or in partnerships with men often tell me this. When lists of tasks are drawn up for a project, the man will automatically take the high-profile tasks. He'll grab tasks as they come up. 'I'll do that one,' he'll say. Women say, 'He wants to be in the limelight while I'm stuck in the background doing research and taking notes!' When men act this way, women assume it means that men think they can do things better themselves.

Lucinda and Alan, sales partners in a software company, were in this typical situation. According to Lucinda, every time they had their weekly sales meeting to decide on goals and tasks, she would listen, thinking about what she could do best before she took on any tasks. In the meantime, though, Alan went ahead and grabbed all the tasks he wanted. He ended up doing presentations to clients, making business cases and brainstorming with clients about new product markets. Lucinda was left doing all the background work and research for Alan. Lucinda assumed that Alan's behaviour was sending a direct message to her: he didn't think she was capable of handling the higher profile tasks. She even suspected that Alan was *afraid* of letting her take this work on because he didn't want to have to pick up the pieces if she failed. 'Alan thinks I can't do anything, so he won't even let me take risks,' she said.

Finding the Blind Spot

I pressed Lucinda to check and see if she had a blind spot. At their next sales meeting, she told Alan, 'I have the assumption that you think I can't do higher profile tasks directly with the client.' What a surprise Lucinda got. Alan had never doubted that she could do these things. It just never occurred to him that he was grabbing the riskier, high-profile work for himself and shutting her out.

How could Alan not see what he was doing? The answer is that he was just acting on instinct. As we have seen, men's working style is action-oriented and results-driven. While women get a sense of contributing from other things like building relationships, men's sense of achievement comes from getting results. That's what makes men feel that they're making their best contribution. And it's a huge blind spot for women, who think there's more behind men's actions than men are telling them.

In private, men reveal their true feelings about women's capabilities. The truth is that many men suspect their women colleagues do the job better than they can. Men say, 'Women are more articulate and more organized. They do their homework and come to meetings better prepared.'

Women have a huge blind spot when they assume men think they are incapable. When men act according to their action-oriented working style, they are not trying to imply that women are incompetent. They are just doing what comes naturally to them. Women have to understand men's style and not let it get to them.

They have to stand up for themselves, and grab some of the work they want instead of waiting for it to be offered to them.

How do you break through your assumptions? They key is active listening. Active listening means you 'check' your assumptions before you jump to conclusions about the behaviour of the other sex. Always make sure you understand the real reasons the other sex is acting a certain way before you take any actions. As you have seen, there's a good chance you have a blind spot. Acting on a blind spot can lead to terrible misunderstandings.

But of course, sometimes it's too late to avoid the conflicts that gender-based misunderstandings lead to. When misunderstandings aren't corrected, they can do more than create tension between employees. Sometimes they turn into fully fledged conflicts, and even discriminatory harassment cases. We will look at this in Chapters 10 and 11, and see how it happens. And you'll learn what you can do to solve those conflicts. But first we need to recognize and understand our strengths.

CHAPTER 9

Understanding Our Strengths

Men and women are very different from each other. In the previous chapters, we've seen how different we are. We don't see the same world when we look around us. We don't hear the same thing when we are listening to the same words. And we don't speak the same language. You've seen the challenges that arise when you don't understand how different the other sex is, and you've seen what you can do to overcome those challenges, and improve your working relationship with the opposite sex.

What you might not know is how advantageous men and women's differences really are – for all businesses, everywhere. When we understand them, our differences are a huge source of strength. In the examples at the beginning of this book, both lawyer Sandra and The Body Shop manager Nathan had special skills their colleagues didn't recognize. If their colleagues had only known how to make use of these special skills, they would have seen how valuable they were.

Sandra could build strong relationships with her clients. She could see problems from angles few of her male colleagues would have imagined. Nathan was skilled at sticking to an agenda, steering meetings to a conclusion and getting on to action. He was able to get to the root of things when his colleagues some-times got bogged down in the details of a problem.

The big challenge in today's working world is to create an environment where both men and women flourish. The way to do that is simple. Learn what men and women's special strengths are, and work out how to put them to use.

Men and women have different approaches to almost all day-to-day activities at work. Both can be valuable. Sometimes the women's approaches will get better results. Sometimes the men's approaches will. The key is flexibility. You have to understand what the differences are, and how each approach can work to advantage in a given situation.

Here are some areas where men and women's approaches and working styles differ. Learn to spot these differences and use them to your advantage. You'll be amazed at the results.

Management Styles

Women typically have a consensus-driven style that focuses on creating relationships as much as on achieving specific objectives. Women tend to be inclusive in their approach to managing. They stay the course until they achieve consensus, making sure they get everyone's opinion before they make a decision. Women also tend to direct others by making suggestions.

Men managers usually see their job as getting everyone else on board. They often make decisions before consulting others. Then they try to convince others to subscribe to their visions. Men's style is typically oriented towards meeting an objective. 'Let's just get it done,' men say. Men tend to direct by telling others what to do, as opposed to suggesting a course of action.

The Benefits of Both Approaches

Women's collaborative approach to managing is extremely effective for brainstorming, for coming up with creative new ideas. Yet men's style is probably more effective in emergency situations, when a decision absolutely must be made and carried out quickly. The point is not that only women should brainstorm and only men should get things done. Each sex should learn to look to the other for input when faced with different business challenges.

Problem Solving

When women take on problem solving, they generally try to make sure all aspects of a problem have been well covered before they take action. Their approach is intuitive and contextual. As you have seen, women tend to get to the bottom of things by talking. They cast a wide net of ideas before arriving at a conclusion. Women also try to build consensus to solve problems, so they explore how possible solutions may affect other people or other areas of a business. Women therefore:

- Collaborate.

- Focus on the long term.

- Take lots of factors into consideration.

- Can juggle several potential solutions.

- Are flexible about a solution until a consensus is reached.

- Are not 'married' to a method and will change approaches if they need to.

Women tend to focus on 'problem', while men focus on 'solving'. Men tend to approach problem solving by rolling up their sleeves and tackling problems in an analytical, linear fashion. They approach problem solving in a factual, detached and action-oriented way, and quickly come up with an action plan. While women's style invites consensus, men's invites debate. Men thus:

- Use factual judgment.

- Debate.

- Stick to the situation at hand.

- Think other factors are irrelevant.

- Look for 'the' solution.

- Stick to their solution.

- When there's a solution, they consider it 'done' and off the list.

The Benefits of Both Approaches

Men's approach to problem solving sets the standard in today's business world, but it has its limitations. Men will benefit if they look for input from their female colleagues, who may see other aspects of a problem, and other ways of solving it. This isn't easy for men because it feels like a waste of time and makes them impatient. And men's style isn't easy for women. To a lot of women, rolling up your sleeves too early feels like cutting corners. I suggest to businesses that their male and female employees try each other's styles of problem solving for a week. When they do, they are amazed at the kinds of result they come up with.

Job Interviews

Women usually see job interviews as opportunities for building rapport. They generally assume that their CV speaks for itself. If it lists their accomplishments, women ask, why would they have to repeat those accomplishments during their interview? Women don't like blowing their own trumpet. They aren't comfortable bragging about what they've done – because for women, it sounds like bragging. Women consider this kind of behaviour to be tacky.

Typically, men's style in interviews is to promote themselves. Even when their accomplishments are written on a CV, men will repeat them and expand on them to demonstrate what they've done in a measurable way. In interviews they don't hesitate to mention who they know, and are quite comfortable saying things like, 'I was the one who broke last year's sales targets.'

What women will often express is areas where they could improve. Men, on the other hand, will avoid doing this at all costs. Men will often say that they can do something whether they can or they can't. They'll sail through an interview, speaking in a finite way, whereas women will qualify their answers; for example, they might say, 'I've never really tried that kind of project, but I'm certainly willing to learn.' Women will expose vulnerability: for them this is honest and a sign of integrity; it's part of being thorough and balanced; it's more credible, and it demonstrates their ability to be self-critical. Men hide vulnerability at all costs, because for them it's a sign of weakness. For men, it's better covered up.

Something that interviewers should bear in mind: women are looking for different things in a job than men are. Women want to get a feel for the place, for how people interact together; they seek to learn what kind of environment it is and whether it suits them. In job interviews, women practise what I call 'intuitive judgment'. They will check to see if there are other women in the company, what they are doing, what their relationship is with the men they're working for – and with.

Men, on the other hand, are very 'factual' in the way they assess a potential job. The question for men is: is this a good strategic move for me? What's my position? What's the salary? Who will I report to – in other words, where will I be in the hierarchy in this office?

The Benefits of Both Approaches

Different interviewing styles are a huge source of misunderstanding between men and women. Men often assume an accomplished person will have the ego to go with it. So when women they interview don't show too much ego, men may wonder why they are playing down their accomplishments. Some men even wonder whether those women doctored their CVs. Women, on the other hand, think if you are accomplished, you can afford to be modest. And they judge men on this. An in-your-face attitude has a real stigma for women. So women will see men as overbearing or unnecessarily boastful. Imagine the kinds of opportunity that are lost when women and men jump to these conclusions without checking their assumptions first.

It's important for both men and women to understand these different styles so that they don't eliminate good candidates because of this misunderstanding.

Performance Evaluations

Most performance evaluations work according to the following logic: 'You've accomplished this, but you need to work on that.' This doesn't work well for women. They are already critical enough of their own shortcomings. They already have an internal dialogue of struggle going on. Women are always scrutinizing themselves. It's part of internalizing things. So pointing out women's weaknesses is not the best way to motivate them. Women need to have their accomplishments clearly articulated. That's what gives them breakthroughs.

Performance evaluations work fine for men because pointing out shortcomings motivates them. One difference is that men don't take evaluations personally like women do.

The Benefits of Both Approaches

Men dread giving performance evaluations to women, because they fear how women will react. My advice to men is for them to acknowledge women's strengths; to personalize the process by saying, 'I really enjoy working with you,' and ask women what they think they need to work on next. You'll be surprised. Most of the time, women will bring up the very points you were afraid to deliver yourself. Men will get better results by asking women about their shortcomings instead of telling them what they are.

Men make breakthroughs through hardships, while women make breakthroughs through validation. Men, if you understand the female paradigms, you will have the advantage of being able to promote and validate women and you'll definitely see the results in women's performance.

Male and Female Behaviour at Meetings

As I have said before, women are comfortable moving away from an agenda. For women, it's part of what you have to do to be thorough. Sometimes the point you have to discuss is so important that it might even change the agenda. Anyway, this kind of freedom makes room for more voices to be heard. It allows people to bring up new points, other research or anything else no one had thought of before.

Men like to stick to the agenda. To them, it seems like the most efficient way to run a meeting. As we have seen, when women allow the conversation to broaden, men think it's because women lack focus.

Men and women both try to obtain results from meetings. But they use different approaches. Men use an authoritative approach while women's traditional approach is to wonder, 'What can I do to contribute?' Women often speak in a higher tone of voice, which doesn't project authority as much. Also, unfortunately, the people who speak the loudest are often the ones who are heard.

Being Heard

Women often complain that their ideas aren't 'heard'. Former American Secretary of State Madeleine Albright once told me that even when she spoke at meetings, her ideas were often ignored. Then a man in the meeting would repeat what she had said almost verbatim and everyone would applaud and tell him he'd made a brilliant point! If this happens to one of the most powerful women I've ever met, it's no surprise it happens to other women.

Men have a style of projecting their voice and sounding determined. In meetings, men tend to take far more air time than women. Women tend to speak in an almost apologetic tone ('Excuse me, if I may. . .') I would never ask women to change their natural style; rather, women should learn to frame their contributions by saying, 'I have three things to say; please hear me out.' That captures the attention of both men and women. Or perhaps, 'I've got this great idea.' Women, you shouldn't give yourselves a headache trying to speak louder, but make sure you frame what you say in such a way that people know they're supposed to pay attention: 'I want your feedback on this,' or, 'Hear me out on this.' This helps women to capture attention in a meeting.

Women should also learn to stand their ground. When there's a lot of controversy or disagreement over a topic, women tend to fold. They make the mistake of thinking that if they have strong feelings about something, the men at the meeting will understand, and take them into consideration. Women will say, 'Isn't the fact that we feel strongly about this enough?' But it's not enough. Women have to make specific requests, 'I request that this or that be done.' They need to remember that men will pay attention to the words and the directions women give, but not to how strongly they feel about the subject. In other words, they need to be clear about what they want.

Chairing

Men in meetings like to take charge and get things going. Often, when women are in all-female meetings, they take turns in chairing. Women just aren't married to the traditional way of running a meeting. When women pass the chair on to someone else in the middle of the meeting, this drives men crazy. Both sexes should be sure to decide up front what method should be used.

The Benefits of Both Approaches

In reality, both men's and women's approaches are useful. And there's no reason you can't use both at once. Men and women should just relax and let each other work on their 'own agenda'. One good technique for managing this is to try to follow the official agenda, but keep women's points on a flip chart. This way, all women's points can be addressed while men get the satisfaction of following a logical order and steering towards a conclusion. Many companies have tried this and it works. Not only does everyone come out of meetings feeling that they've been heard, but the meetings are usually more productive.

Selling

Women tend not to sell themselves. What they do is take an interest in their clients. Women like to build trust with their clients, and build long-term relationships. Statistics show that they are very adept at getting repeat business. This means women can walk out of a sales situation empty handed, but still feel that they've achieved something. The 'win' for women is to build rapport with clients and get results.

The 'win' for men is usually to get results. For men, it's like going in for the kill. Men are more focused on closing the sale. They get satisfaction by going in with an objective, and coming out with a result.

Women are better at reading people, so, for example, they'll read when a sale is not going well, and may change gear, offer another product or ask the client open-ended questions like 'Would there be something else that would be more suitable?' Women make connections to people, while men make object-focused connections to stories – like the story of a conquest.

The Benefits of Both Approaches

It's good to have gender balance in a sales team so you can use both approaches. Studies show that women are as good at reading men as they are at reading women, while men are only good at reading men. So men should look to their female colleagues for insight on women.

When men and women go on joint sales calls, they should be ready to use both approaches, depending on the client. With their strict focus on results, men risk missing important details about a client's expectations or needs. Let women lead the way on this, and they'll work it out in no time. The real challenge is for both men and women to avoid stepping on each other's toes.

If they can evaluate a client's needs and expectations, they can let the person with the most effective technique take the lead.

Men should just bear in mind that 'closing the sale' is not the only thing that's important to women. And women should bear in mind that for men, it is.

Delegating

Women tend to have a hard time delegating. They take on a lot at work. Many women get bogged down by detail work, or by doing research they could hand over to someone else. The result? Women often feel overwhelmed and overworked.

Men are more comfortable delegating tasks to others. They also have a strong ability to simplify things. They'll slim things down by saying, 'Let's just focus on these three things.' Women are more trusting about sharing information than men, but when it comes to workload, they are not as comfortable just handing work over, especially the 'grunt work'. It's the methodology of it, really. Men have an easier time handing over work, probably because they are socialized to give orders.

In cross-mentoring, women find that when they are mentored by a man in this area, they learn to delegate better.

The Benefits of Both Approaches

Women can learn a lot from men. They should look at the way men comfortably make requests of others. To women, this feels like asking others to do their work for them. But it's not. In most cases, things can be simplified and women can greatly reduce their workload while still achieving good results. When women emulate men's delegation style, they are surprised what a load it takes off their shoulders.

Negotiation

Women have an ability to negotiate in an inclusive way. They naturally tend to hear everyone out. Studies have shown that women retain this ability, even in crisis situations. Women use 'exploring ideas' as a form of negotiation. They'll ask, 'Have you considered this way of looking at the issue?' This style has the effect of making people pause and relax, and often makes people more open to compromise. Women are sociologically brought up to be peacemakers. They validate situations so people feel heard. They defuse the debate. Women will:

- Use more open questions, like 'How do you feel about this?'

- Keep the tone collegial while they build a relationship and make it stronger.

- Use a collaborative style, saying 'Let's explore this.'

- Validate the other's position. 'You look at it that way. I look at it this way.'

- Show flexibility.

- Look for a collaborative, flexible, win-win solution. They will give and take.

Men tend to escalate the debate. They tend to play devil's advocate, and approach negotiation with a linear style. They treat it as a see-saw process. 'I make my demands. The other party makes its demands, and eventually we agree on something.' Men see negotiating as a matter of competing for position. They go in with a goal in mind and drive to achieve it. Men will:

- Use more action-oriented, closed questions, like 'What do you want?'

- Speak in finite terms about what they've agreed on; for example, they'll say, 'so far we've decided this.'

- Look for closure.

- Use an argumentative style.

- Show consistency.

- Agree to disagree.

The Benefits of Both Approaches

Like selling, negotiating is a fine art. Different countries and cultures have their own rules. So it's good to enter negotiations with as many strategies at your disposal as possible. Women's style achieves results too, and often better results. But sometimes men's approach is more effective. Men and women negotiating together should be aware of their different styles and be willing to adapt to the circumstances they find themselves in. Sometimes sticking to your own demands is a good idea. But sometimes the more seductive approach is good too. Men and women can easily learn their respective styles by watching each other negotiate in different circumstances.

Networking

For women, networking is a good opportunity to build ongoing relationships and lasting support bases. Women feel a sense of bonding when they're networking. They'll stay in a group for a long time instead of skipping from one person to the next. Women often network with no particular objective in mind. They feel it's rude and even tacky to network in a self-serving and transparent manner. Women:

- Use 'web' thinking; they create a series of networks that inter-connect.

- Constantly nurture those networks, even though it's not a means to a specific end.

- Often just have a hunch that something fruitful will come out of a relationship.

- Will juggle relationships that don't necessarily have anything to do with one another.

- Often network just to learn something new.

Men move around a lot when they are in a networking situation. For them, networking is usually done with a specific purpose in mind. It's a means to an end. Men want to meet specific contacts for specific reasons. Men:

- Become members of clubs either for status or to get connections as a means to a specific end.

- Cultivate a variety of networks: they have friends who they socialize with; people who they go fishing or golfing with, and acquaintances who may enhance their results in business.

Both women's and men's networks are 'fluid', in that a new contact is often introduced to an existing network acquaintance, who may then add the new 'name' to their own network.

The Benefits of Both Approaches

Men and women can both learn from watching each other network. Because of their open-ended networking style, women sometimes lose out on great opportunities. They are afraid of appearing too purposeful when they meet people. But women can shed some of that hesitation by watching a male colleague work a room. Of course, men's results-driven networking style means they run the risk of alienating people – especially women. By watching women network, men can pick up tips for building rapport and long-term relationships. Sometimes these things are more valuable than short-term results.

One more hint to both sexes: women continue networking by maintaining personal contact with others, sending a personal message via e-mail or voicemail every so often, or making a useful introduction. Men usually stay in touch by sending things: documents, newspaper articles or web links. Women should not be offended if the men they network don't phone them. That's what men are doing by sending an interesting article. But men should remember that a personal communication with women will go a long way in solidifying the relationship. It doesn't take much effort, and the results last forever.

Public Speaking

Women tend to approach speaking engagements as dialogues. They often appear to audiences more as facilitators than as presenters. Women are not as comfortable 'pontificating' when they speak. Rather, they tend to invite listeners to participate and ask questions. They like to be entertaining, engaging and inviting when they speak.

Men usually follow the traditional 'declarative' style of public speaking: articulate an argument, restate it, summarize it, wrap it up, then wait for the applause. Men tend to want to keep questions under control. They'd rather get people to subscribe to their argument than give them feedback on it.

There is a stereotypical assumption about what makes a good public speaker: a convincing, authoritative storyteller who is in control of the audience. That tends to be more of a male approach.

The snag is that women who conform to this approach are inter-preted as being too forceful, unapproachable and arrogant. The women who have established themselves – who are powerful, well-known experts or have big names – are freed from this and can express themselves authentically. They are seen as far more engaging and inquisitive, and create more dialogue; they 'ask more rather than tell more', and are ' "humorous" as opposed to "telling jokes".'

What can the average woman do to break out of this syn-drome of not being taken seriously? Women are very articulate – they need to use this attribute. It's a powerful framing tool, so use it to directly establish your own credibility. Say, 'I have an absolutely indisputable, convincing argument here' or, 'I have twenty years experience . . .' This will create the same kind of attention in the audience, but by using language rather than adopting a 'male style'. Then you can use your own authentic, engaging, inquisitive speaking style.

The Benefits of Both Approaches

If you want to have a participatory event, where people will listen and feel comfortable giving their points of view, you had better get a woman to design it. It's worth taking the time to decide what kind of presentation you want to deliver. Studies show that people are tired of the traditional presentation style. In other words, people are tired of being talked at. So men can learn a lot from women's approach to making presentations and speeches.

You may have heard the old saying: 'When men speak people listen. When women speak, people look. If they like what they see, they listen.' Unfortunately, in today's business world, this still holds true. So women have to go the extra distance to get cred-ibility when they speak. Women's natural 'participatory' public speaking style may not help them in all situations. So they would do well to watch men's style.

Both sexes should gauge the nature of the presentation they have to make, and take their cues from each other.

Giving Promotions

We tend to promote people who are like us, and only promote people who are unlike us when they emulate us. This goes for men and for women – except that until recently, men have done most of the promoting in the working world. The result was a pattern where men promoted men on their potential, but only promoted women for their accomplishments. Men don't do this deliberately. It's about their 'comfort zone'.

It's because men tend to network with men, so that they don't get to know women as well as they do men. To alleviate this situation, men don't need to leave the networks they have, but they should either invite women into their networks, or learn to go out of their comfort zone into networks where there are more women. That's the only way men will get to know women, and understand the unique strengths women bring to business.

The challenge for all businesses and individual managers is to learn to be more inclusive, not only in employing people, but also in giving promotions. And the way to do that is to expand your ideas about what qualities employees need, to be 'right' for the job. When you are taking someone on, scrutinize your decisions to see if you are choosing the person who is most like you, or the person who is best for the job. We are all limiting ourselves by promoting 'likeness'. As you have seen, there is strength in difference.

Look to the Other

I learned about the advantage of combining men and women's perspectives first hand with a former client. Looking back on it now, this personal breakthrough had a huge influence on my life. It is one of the reasons I do the work I do today.

It all started with one relatively small incident. I had been working for months on a sales contract for this client. At first I thought I had a great relationship with them, but slowly I began to doubt this. The more work I did, the more they asked me to do extra work that wasn't part of our contract. One day my frustration reached boiling point, so I went looking for some sympathy from one of my male colleagues. I was starting to feel genuinely hurt by this client's behaviour. 'Why would they think they could take advantage of me like this?' I asked him.

Coming from his male perspective, my colleague had a completely different assessment of the situation. I went to him for sympathy but what I got was a solution. He said, 'Maybe they're not deliberately taking advantage of you. Maybe they just love your work. Instead of getting angry with your client, why don't you just go back to the contract and try to make an amendment so that you will be compensated for your extra time?' I acted on his advice and faxed the new contract to the client with my request. They agreed to my terms. I solved the problem in half an hour, and probably saved weeks or even months of self-questioning. It probably saved my relationship with that client too.

Sometimes getting an opinion from a member of the opposite sex can be very helpful. Both women and men would gain a lot from following this advice. The fact that men don't tend to take things as personally can be a boost when women want a different perspective on a problem. I often turn to male colleagues and associates when I'm feeling overwhelmed by the implications of a problem. Quite often, they help me to stop wondering if things are my fault. They help me to stop mulling things over and to start looking for solutions.

There are also lots of ways in which women's viewpoints can help men to deal with a problem. A former client who is a manager at IBM tells me he never makes major decisions now without consulting at least two women. 'Women's multi-thinking often helps me to see all the implications of a problem, so I can judge better if a solution is going to be effective,' he says.

Clients who have participated in this work often call me up to tell me stories of breakthroughs they had when they got a new perspective from a male or female colleague. One man, a manager at an investment firm, says women's input saved him from a very big mistake. There were two women on his advisory board when he was approached by an Internet start-up company looking for financing. The company wined and dined him and presented a thorough business plan. He was sold on the idea, but the two women on his board were hesitant. They told him there was something wrong. They couldn't put their finger on it exactly, but something in the story of the relationship the company had with other firms didn't add up. The other men on the board said, 'It's not an issue.' But my client wisely gave the women the time to follow through their hunch.

The Internet company had emphasized the number of contracts it already had with major companies, but something in its language sounded vague. The women decided to telephone all the clients to check if the Internet company was really working for them. It turned out that contracts for eight of the ten projects in the Internet company's business plan had not actually been signed. Women's 'exploratory' thinking saved the investment firm a lot of money.

In another story, a member of a law society told me about the society's project to locate firms who were exemplary in terms of gender equality, in order to promote this among their members. They automatically focused on large law firms, thinking people would pay more attention to these firms. But then several women involved in the project – those who had done their homework – pointed out that 90 per cent of law firms were actually small. The women argued that examples of small firms who excelled in gender equality would be more meaningful to the majority of law firms – and the majority of lawyers.

But of course, the road runs in two directions. Women's multi-thinking can lead them to situations where they can't see their way out of problems. Pondering over problems and revisiting them can bring new angles that lead to solutions, but can also make problems seem overwhelmingly complex. Typically, when women find themselves in this situation, they turn to colleagues for advice. Actually, they contact them in order to 'talk about it'. If those colleagues are men, they tend to respond with solutions. And as we have seen, solutions often backfire on women. Women interpret men's behaviour as dismissive.

I recommend that women anticipate the type of reaction they'll get from men and mine the gold. Women have to remember that when men give solutions, they are giving top-quality goods. Men's perspective can make women stop pondering over problems and help them to act when it's time to act.

Converting Differences into Strengths

The truth is, we can no longer afford to get stuck in the traditional business model we saw in Chapter 1. We created a machine that worked well in the past, but it doesn't work any more. Businesses need to learn to be flexible and understand how men and women are different. And then they need to use those differences to their advantage. For the most part, this means including the attributes women bring to the workplace instead of seeing those qualities as obstacles. Daniel Goleman (author of *Emotional Intelligence*), makes the point that we create business from an old paradigm. His argument is that typical female attributes are more necessary than ever in today's business environment where, to get ahead, we rely less on linear, analytical thinking and more on emotional intelligence.

The following chart summarizes men and women's different strengths.

Women	Men
Rapport talk	Report talk
Collaborative	Competitive
Suggestive	Directive
Internalizes	Externalizes
Connected	Detached
Contextual	Specific
Flexible	Consistent
Intuitive	Factual
Networks for relationships	Networks for connections
Validates	Debates

What we have to do is look for the approach that is appropriate and effective for different circumstances. Historically, we've depended on the right side of the chart. When women entered the workplace, we tried to clone those 'right-side' qualities on to both genders. What a waste of skills and talents. If you choose to draw from both sides of the chart, you'll be amazed at the kind of breakthroughs you'll achieve, both personally and for your company.

Things are Changing

I'm happy to report that there are many companies that have learned to put the strengths of both sexes to work for them. And the result was that the environment changed. They changed the water in their fish tank and the individuals in it flourished. Changing the water so it suits everyone is a big job, and a long-term commitment, but I can feel the change at many of the companies I have worked with. Before organizations start working on gender awareness, the men working there tend to be guarded. The women feel they have to struggle to be taken seriously. After the organizations have made a serious commitment to gender awareness, their working environments become inviting, welcoming, collaborative and fun.

I have particularly noticed changes in sales and consulting businesses I have worked with. In many of these companies the macho boardroom environment has just vanished. What I see in its place is a culture of 'clusters', where co-workers team up to work on problems collaboratively. One company has introduced formal brainstorming sessions. The rule is that everyone – including new employees – can take the floor, talk about a problem, give their advice and say what's on their mind. In a genuinely collaborative atmosphere, people feel comfortable and they speak up. And sometimes they have brilliant ideas.

One small change in an investment firm struck me as particularly significant. I recall that the first time I visited the firm, its cafeteria was strictly segregated: there was one long table for senior management and no one else sat at it, even if it was empty. The last time I visited the company the table had gone. Everyone was making an effort to sit with someone new every day. The president told me he sits down to eat with the janitor every now and again, 'just to see what's going on.'

I invite companies to try to get a discussion going about gender difference. Some companies have found some truly ingenious ways to do this. One firm started a cross-gender mentoring and 'buddy' system. When employees need a new perspective on an issue, they call up their buddy: men and women interact by e-mail or phone, or have lunch together. They bounce ideas, problems and business challenges off each other and find that – in a casual and informal way – this exchange of views from different angles enhances their work. They also learn how to communicate more effectively with the other gender. Mentoring, on the other hand, is hierarchically structured, the mentor being an experienced and more senior employee.

Some companies have ongoing cross-gender lunches where employees can exchange perspectives and talk about gender difference. One president I know systematically consults a senior female executive and a female middle manager before he makes decisions – just to get their insights and opinions.

If you are a manager or supervisor, the important thing to understand is that in order to introduce change, you've got to mean it. Women have a perception that gender equality is just the flavour of the month. They believe their companies are addressing gender issues because everyone else is, or because they want to project an image of being progressive, people-friendly places to work for. These women don't believe the will to change is really there. And in many cases, they're right. The will to change isn't here.

It is essential to turn a no-win situation into a win-win situation. Gaining gender awareness will make everyone feel happier and more valued. Deep down that's what everyone wants. Yet unfortunately, there are some obstacles that may still prevent companies from reaching this goal. In the next two chapters, we'll look at how conflicts unfold, how sexual harassment can ruin the working environment of a company, and how you can avoid and overcome such situations.

CHAPTER 10

Resolving Gender Conflicts

What matters most is how we respond to what we experience in life.

Victor Frankl, author, *Man's Search for Meaning*

Men and women have different styles and approaches to most of the tasks we perform in an average working day. Once you understand those differences, you can easily turn them to your advantage. But when it comes to workplace conflicts, we all lose sight of this strength in being different.

Part of the problem is that when it comes to conflict, men and women literally come from two different worlds. Women see conflict as a breakdown. They view it as corrosive. One reason for this is that women internalize, and the conflict automatically becomes personal. For men, conflict is not so much a breakdown as a struggle. Men tend to view conflict as a challenge, a contest to be won. It's a call to battle.

Men and women don't deal with conflict the same way either. Women's first reaction to conflict is to personalize it. They wonder, 'What did I do?' Men tend to treat conflict in an isolated, depersonalized manner. For women, it's about the relationship. That's one reason women tend to approach a conflict by treating it as an opportunity, a chance to have a clear-out, build rapport and get closer in the relationship. Women's instinct is to explore a conflict, figuring out how the conflict or its solution might affect other parties. Women ask others to get to the bottom of the problem by sharing their feelings. Men, on the other hand, tend to react to conflict by staking out a position – much the way they do when they negotiate. At work, they typically bark orders to others in a directive, here's-what-we're-going-to-do manner.

What do men and women in conflict have in common? Conflicts always start at the same source: unmet expectations. When our expectations are not met – for example when someone hasn't done the job they promised to do, or the one we expected – we are surprised. The impact of the unfulfilled promise hits us and we have a reaction: frustration, uncertainty or anger. Men and women both go through this basic reaction to conflict. It's almost universal. But after that, men and women head off in different directions.

We all know what happens after men have experienced the basic surprise of conflict. Men typically explode. They instinctively and instantly look outside to someone or something else. They'll show anger and direct it at that someone or something. They'll slam their fist on a table or yell. It's the way they let their stress out.

Women usually find this reaction perplexing, and even frightening. But that's because women's own way of reacting to conflict is almost the opposite. Women implode. When they find themselves in a conflict, the first question women tend to ask is, 'What have I done wrong?' This doesn't mean they aren't angry. Women hold their reaction in while they try to make sense of it. They're working on their reaction, inside. They ponder, mull it over – even if it's only briefly. Then they may have an emotional reaction, sometimes to the point of crying. Men find this perplexing because they think tears are a sign of sadness. They often tell me tears make them feel helpless. But, as we've seen, tears, at work, are almost always an expression of frustration and anger.

Many experts in different disciplines see these basic differences in different terms. Linguist Walter Ong points out in *Fighting for Life* that men's reaction to conflict is part of a set of ritualized behaviours that includes contests, competition, struggle and contention. Women, he says, tend to fight for real rather than ritualized purposes.[1] Paleopsychologist (cultural psychologist) Howard Bloom, author of *The Global Brain*, writes that in organizations, men spend more time posturing, or in hierarchical displays or territorial competitions. When women deal with conflicts, he writes, they 'dig in, find solutions and get back to work.' So although women may be less purely results-oriented than men are in many aspects of working life, when it comes to conflict, Bloom says they are 'more goal-oriented and less political.'[2]

Attacking versus Resolving

It's not that women are afraid of conflict. They just don't like conflict for conflict's sake. Working women often ask me, 'Why do we have to have all this debate at the office all the time?' Women see debate and arguing as 'attacking'. Women also say they find men locked in their position or inflexible when they deal with conflicts. But that's because women assume, from the start, that the way to solve conflicts is through conciliation. For women, winning is not usually the real point.

Linguist Deborah Tannen in her recent book, *The Argument Culture*, writes that women at work are frequently puzzled by how men can argue with each other and then continue as if nothing has happened.[3] Men at work are often surprised when women are deeply upset by a verbal attack. For men, it's simply part of getting the job done. But women often wonder, 'Why does he have to jump all over me like that?' It is common for men to use ritual opposition even where there is no real conflict, such as teasing, playfully insulting each other, or exploring ideas by playing devil's advocate. This approach creates tension and conflict between women and men at work. Many women avoid overt disagreement when they really do disagree, because conflict for them signals a breakdown.

According to psychologists John Gottman and Robert Levenson at the University of Washington, you can see the differences in how men and women react to conflict by simply observing the physiological changes conflict provokes. The pair asked male and female patients to identify and discuss a major area of disagreement in their marriage. While the patients were doing this, they monitored factors like their heart rates, blood flow, skin temperature and body movements. What did they find?

Men literally get more 'heated up' and physically stimulated by conflict. Women experience less physical change during sustained conflict. Their conclusion: men need to shut off or cool down during conflict or they get overwhelmed and lose control, while women can tolerate longer, escalating bouts of conflict without losing control.[4]

So How Can We Resolve Conflicts?

Most of us know how to resolve conflicts. We get advice like 'Explain your viewpoint' or 'Be very clear, consistent and direct.' Most of us go through our careers assuming that this is all there is to do. And we think it's probably enough. Of course, if we looked around and made a tally of the number of continuing conflicts we see or hear about in an average week at the office, we might start to wonder just how efficient those good old methods for solving conflicts really are.

I can tell you – from the number of conflicts I'm called in to deal with in an average week – that the good old methods don't work. And they don't work because we all overlook a few basic things about the nature of conflicts.

We've seen in previous chapters how men and women each assume that the other sex thinks like they do. So they project their own reactions onto those of the other sex. In conflict, men and women do the same thing: they assume the other sex hears the same words and speaks the same language as they do. But of course, men and women don't speak the same language. Their words and actions don't necessarily mean the same thing. So, unless you recognize how your actions appear to the other sex, your reaction will only make things worse.

This syndrome of misunderstandings is as common at work as it is at home. One of my Canadian associates, Brenda, told me this story of a typical conflict she and her husband got into over cooking together. Their kitchen was small, so it wasn't easy to cook together, but that day, things were going particularly smoothly. Then, according to Brenda, 'Jacques hit his head by accident on a cupboard door. And how did he react? He slammed it shut and cursed!' Brenda was mystified and hurt. To her, the reaction seemed completely out of proportion with the accident – which was just a result of Jacques' own carelessness. 'Why does he have to take out his anger on a cupboard door?' Like most women Brenda took her husband's expression of anger personally. It felt like a personal attack to her. The way she saw it, Jacques stole a good moment from her. They were cooking peacefully and he went and ruined it by over-reacting to what looked like a pretty minor incident to her. She told him what she thought.

Jacques simply didn't understand why Brenda was hurt and offended by his outburst. He told her it was just his way of letting off steam. 'It's got nothing to do with you,' he said. But to Brenda, it did have something to do with her. She persisted in resenting his reaction. Jacques was confused and frustrated. They both felt misunderstood. She was stuck in her position: 'You over-reacted.' And he was stuck in his: 'It had nothing to do with you.'

And by this point, neither of them felt like being in the same room – let alone like cooking together in a tiny kitchen.

This is a classic dynamic between men and women in conflict. The more men explode, the more women implode. When women personalize situations, men's frustration meter rises; they feel they're being accused of something they didn't intend. 'It's not about you.' When women hear this, they tend to shut down because they also feel they're not being understood.

It happens at work all the time. One of my clients, Marylin, called me with a typical male-female work conflict situation. She was convinced that her boss, Ray, was being abusive towards her. By the time she called me, she was on the verge of hiring a lawyer to sue him. I asked her where this feeling came from. 'In almost every e-mail he sends he clearly appears to me to be angry!' Marylin felt that the e-mails were attacks. I suspected she was misinterpreting Ray's style, so I asked her if I could read them myself. The style of the e-mails was clearly 'directive'. After a brief conversation with her boss, Marylin realized she had made a big assumption. Ray wasn't attacking her. His directive style just sounded that way to her. In just one quick meeting, she and her boss resolved the misunderstanding. E-mails can be a major cause of communication breakdown as our dependence on electronic coversations grows. Try to avoid having an argument this way – one that is meticulously documented, and that you may regret. Pick up the telephone before the situation can escalate.

The challenge in conflicts – as in all your dealings with the opposite sex – is to avoid becoming a victim of your own faulty assumptions. To avoid this fate, the first thing you need is S.A.R.A.

S.A.R.A.

I learned a great lesson about how we react to conflict situations from a famous psychologist I once studied with, Virginia Satir.

She said that people go through four stages when they are in a conflict: Surprise, Anger, Rejection and Acceptance.[5] I call this S.A.R.A. Some people go through every stage. Others skip some stages. Some people are Surprised, but go straight to Acceptance without passing through Anger. These are all normal human reactions, and nothing to be ashamed about. In fact, it's better to have these reactions and recognize them for what they are than to pretend you don't have them. You'll soon see why.

Without realizing it, most people get stuck in either Anger or Rejection. Where you get stuck partly depends on gender. Men tend to get stuck in Anger, projecting their reaction to conflict in an outwards direction. Not surprisingly, women tend to get stuck in Rejection, because they project their reaction to conflict inwards. Women tend to internalize conflict.

The problem is that when men are stuck in Anger and women are stuck in Rejection, their reactions reinforce one another. Perceptual filters kick in again. In Rejection, women say, 'It's not my fault!' This triggers men's anger because men feel they're being blamed. When men react defensively, they retrigger women's feeling of Rejection. That makes women feel men don't want to listen to them, and feeds that feeling even more.

This syndrome where men and women's reactions reinforce each other doesn't help the ultimate problem both sexes face: getting to Acceptance. Why is this so important? When we are stuck in Surprise, Anger or Rejection, it is too early to act. You can't do anything productive to resolve a conflict. That's why it's good to recognize the stages. Then you need to take whatever time you need to get to Acceptance.

Suffer in the Short Term

Getting to Acceptance is a matter of intentions. I often tell people, 'It can take five minutes or it can take five years. You decide. But it has to be done.' How do you get to Acceptance? The best way is to remind yourself of your long-term intentions. Our long-term intentions are the first thing we forget about when we're in a conflict. But they're usually more important than being 'right'. That means you have to accept some short-term suffering.

A young accountant, David, told me a story that perfectly illustrates why it's so important to get over Anger and Rejection before doing anything about a conflict. Many people will relate to this phone message scenario. David was head of a team of 18 accountants working on a tax return for a large company. While he was on a business trip his team leader left him three messages warning him that they were probably not going to make the deadline. The team was having difficulty getting the information it needed from the client. On his way back from his trip David picked up one last message from his answering machine. This time it was from the client. The president accused David of being unprofessional because David's team was clearly behind schedule. 'We are one of your largest clients,' he said. 'And this shows us we're not really that important to you.'

'I was stunned,' David recalled. 'I knew it wasn't our fault and it certainly wasn't my fault! I remember I was on the pavement holding my mobile, pacing backwards and forwards. Then I just jabbed the callback button and unloaded on his voicemail. It was a knee-jerk reaction.' As soon as David ended the call he knew he had made a mistake. 'I thought about it for a second and realized there was probably a misunderstanding. There was probably a communication problem somewhere. I wished so much I could get into the president's voicemail and delete my message.'

It turned out that a communication problem was at the root of the misunderstanding. David's team had been trying to get information from the company. The team leader had left repeated messages for the client but had not received any response. As it turned out, the company had received the messages. They didn't answer them. They just acted on them. They were busy getting the information together. It was just taking longer than they expected. But David didn't know that. And the company's president didn't know it either. Each saw the delay and automatically assumed it was the other's fault. 'It wasn't really anyone's fault,' David said.

There are two ways of dealing with conflicts. Before we get to Acceptance we act in what I call 'Blame Frame'. This is a win-lose mindset. When you are in Blame Frame, you are attached to your opinion. You are attached to being right. Your objective is to prove the other person wrong. When you are in the Outcome Frame, your goal is to find real resolution. Your objective is to find a win-win solution that will make everyone happy. Lots of people in conflict think it is unrealistic to have a win-win solution. They think someone has to lose. That's just because they are in the Blame Frame.

When you are in Surprise, Anger or Rejection, you're probably operating in the Blame Frame, and when you're in the Blame Frame, it's too early to act.

Blaming is a normal human reaction. No one likes conflicts and when they happen, the first thing we think about is ourselves. We want to pin the fault on someone else. But that's the problem with trying to resolve a conflict when you are in the Blame Frame. It's about fault-finding, not solution-finding. It's about 'you or me'. It's zero-sum, win or lose, 'I'm right and you're wrong.' Most people assume you solve conflicts by talking. But talking won't solve anything if you're in the Blame Frame. It only digs you in deeper. You're still trying to decide who is at fault.

David's story is a perfect example. David was in Blame Frame when he made the snap decision to call the president and unload on him. When David felt attacked, he reacted by attacking back. He may have felt momentary relief after speaking his mind to the president's voicemail, but that didn't do much to solve the problem. He understood that pretty quickly.

After David left the first message, he cooled down a bit, got over his Anger and decided to look for a win-win solution. David was in Acceptance. He was ready for the Outcome Frame. He started by checking his assumptions. He made a few calls to find out how the misunderstanding had occurred. He quickly realized that everyone was acting in good faith. So he called the president back and explained the situation. They agreed that it was no one's fault and extended the deadline for the tax return. Problem solved.

The Win-Win Way – Outcome Frame

The only way to resolve a conflict is to change from the Blame Frame to the Outcome Frame. This means switching your frame of reference from fault-finding to solution-finding. These five tips will help you:

1. Have a break. Remove yourself. Say, 'I'll come back to you on that.' Personally, I give myself five minutes to do this. I do it on my own. You can also go and see someone else, if you need to.

2. If you see someone else, may sure they are a committed listener, not just an 'ear'. Don't just go to someone for sympathy or you'll end up stuck back in the Blame Frame. It's sensible to choose someone with a completely differently perspective from your own, maybe even someone you don't know that well. Present that person with your challenge and explain what you're looking for.

3. Get in touch with your long-term intentions. Are you committed to working with this client/colleague/partner? Do you want to make a partnership or collaboration work? If the answer is 'Yes', then you need to ask a few simple questions.

How can we resolve this? What would be an ideal solution for you?

4. Forget about who's right and who's wrong and focus on the cost of the conflict. To do THAT you have to be in Acceptance. You have to get over thinking of 'being right'.

5. Detach yourself from your opinions, because the first step in resolving conflicts through the Outcome Frame is to find out what a 'winning' solution would be for the other side.

When you follow these basic steps, your hostilities usually melt away and the solution will follow.

The following story of a conflict at an engineering firm shows how you can move from the Blame Frame to the Outcome Frame – and how easy it is to find a solution once you're in the Outcome Frame. The story involves two colleagues, Gordon, a partner at the firm, and Sylvia, the accounts manager. Gordon had received a call from one of their most important clients who insisted they needed a contract finished for the next day. He was still feeling the shock of that when he went to talk to Sylvia at 3 p.m. 'It absolutely has to be done for tomorrow,' he said. 'We don't have a choice.' That really put Sylvia on the spot. She had promised her husband she would pick up the children from a nursery that afternoon at 5 p.m. 'I'll work on it for the next two hours, but I absolutely have to be away by 5 p.m.,' she said.

Gordon's reaction? 'It absolutely has to be done by tomorrow.'

Sylvia was shocked but she tried a compromise. 'I'll try to get a babysitter, and if I can, I'll come back tonight and work on it. But I can't make any promises,' she said.

That just made Gordon angrier. He blurted out in frustration, 'Oh, not the children again! It's just impossible for it to wait. I promised it would be on the client's desk tomorrow morning.'

The sarcastic comment about her children really hurt Sylvia. Gordon's words put her on the defensive. Conflicts like these are of what I call the jugular variety. They get people by the throat by dragging up sensitive issues. They aren't easy to defuse. They bring out emotions we didn't know we had, and trigger things we're not even aware of. They are the kinds of conflict that 'raise every antenna'.

But even these kinds of conflict can be solved by switching from the Blame Frame to the Outcome Frame. Gordon was stuck in Anger and Sylvia was stuck in feeling Rejection. After they got over their reactions and got into Acceptance, they were able to move towards finding a solution. Gordon started by taking ownership of his request. He told Sylvia, 'I am having a huge problem with this client. They absolutely insist on having this report done by tomorrow morning and I promised they would have it. Is there a way we can meet this deadline?'

Sylvia dropped her defences. Gordon's approach put her in a problem-solving, outcome mode. Sylvia knew the client. She knew they often made these kinds of last minute demands. And she knew that after they got their reports, they let them sit for three weeks before they did anything with them. She explained this to Gordon. 'I know this client makes a lot of demands. But I also know that if I push, they'll give a bit. It usually doesn't turn out to be a problem when we can't do things as quickly as they want.'

When Gordon heard this he understood something about his earlier reaction to the client's request. He explained to Sylvia that he was from the old school, where the customer is king. Sylvia explained her point of view. She said that her team would do a better job if they had a reasonable amount of time. 'The overall outcome will be better,' she said. They agreed that if she worked a few hours from home at the weekend, then finished the rest early in the week, without rushing the job, the client would probably be happier. They were.

Team Conflicts

An office equipment company once approached me for advice on how to deal with another of these 'jugular' conflicts between three of its sales representatives. The conflict started when the three – two women and one man – went to make a presentation to a potential client. The stakes were high. The contract was one of the biggest the company had ever seen. Greg made the presentation and they lost the contract. That's when the conflict started. The two women, June and Caroline, blamed Greg for blowing it.

Greg didn't think it was his fault. He said he just did his stuff. This was Greg's version of events: he was making a presentation to the senior manager (a man) and three women who worked for him. And he just followed his instinct. Without even thinking about it, he zeroed in on the male manager. Later, Greg reported, 'I just gave him the facts. I told him we had the best product at the best price and he was guaranteed satisfaction. And I did a great job.' Greg didn't have a clue what went wrong.

But June and Caroline certainly did! They said Greg had gone downhill all the way from the minute he opened his mouth. 'It was obviously the women who were making the decision,' they explained. 'And Greg didn't pay any attention to them.' Their competitors took a much softer approach to the sale and June and Caroline could see it was working.

'You blew it,' they told Greg after the presentations. Greg wouldn't hear of it. 'No. I did a terrific job!'

The team lost the sale, but that wasn't the real problem. The real problem was that the incident had sparked a conflict between them that no one seemed able to resolve. That was when their sales director came to see me.

The first thing I did was listen to everyone's version of events. June and Caroline said that right from the start they had seen Greg's approach wasn't working. 'You came across as overbearing and condescending,' they told him. 'The women in the room could tell that the only one you thought you had to convince was their boss, and they were turned off.' Greg reacted defensively. 'You can't blame *me*. I did a perfect job.' He said that he thought everyone was plotting against him. June and Caroline said he refused to listen to them. They were in a deadlock.

Greg, June and Caroline's dispute shows how easy it is to fall into the Blame Frame. 'We saw that Greg was losing the client right away,' they told me. 'After that we just saw a checklist of what was going wrong, of the mistakes he was making.' In other words, June and Caroline's Blame Frame shaped the way they saw Greg's whole presentation.

Greg was in the Blame Frame too. He said his only thoughts about the whole incident were that 'June and Caroline are ganging up on me.' He felt like a victim, as if they were gathering evidence against him. 'It's not my fault. It's their fault.' And what did he do? He stopped listening to them. He shut down. June and Caroline, meanwhile, assumed Greg just wasn't listening. Their reactions reinforced one another.

There isn't much that can be done to avoid going through the Blame Frame. It's all part of the normal human reaction to conflict situations. The problem is that when you are in the Blame Frame, you aren't ready to do anything to really resolve a conflict. You can't resolve conflicts when you are focused on having your own position understood. What you have to be able to say is: 'I want to understand the other person.'

Greg, June and Caroline had to wait a few weeks before they were ready to move from the Blame Frame to the Outcome Frame. How did they do this? They started by recalling what their long-term goals were. As I've said before, the first thing that goes out of the window when we are in a conflict is our long-term intention. As soon as Greg and June and Caroline were in a conflict situation, they just forgot they were a good team.

I asked them, 'What's the cost of being in the Blame Frame?'

It didn't take them long to come up with an answer. They lost trust in one another, they said. And they lost the special chemistry that had made them a good team. As they would later see, being in the Blame Frame was probably what lost them their client too. 'What are you all committed to?' I asked them. Again, it didn't take them long to come up with an answer. 'Being a strong team. That's how we win clients,' they answered. When they all heard themselves saying the same thing, the dispute suddenly went from 'it's you against me' to 'it's you *and* me'.

That's when Greg, June and Caroline switched from the Blame Frame to the Outcome Frame. Then the past event took on a whole new meaning for them. Each saw what they could have done to save the situation. 'I have a confession to make,' said Caroline. 'I knew the women in the room would have the last word on the purchase. I could have jumped in and steered your attention to them. But instead, I just watched your presentation ticking like a time bomb.' In the Blame Frame, Greg saw that he would have shut that kind of interruption out. But in the Outcome Frame he would have welcomed it. He would have realized Caroline had a reason for doing what she was doing.

Once we got to the Outcome Frame and resolved their conflict, Greg, June and Caroline all had an insight about turning their differences into strengths. All three saw what they lost because they were stuck in the Blame Frame: not only the client, but also their trust in each other. Greg realized he could have had a lot of help from June and Caroline if he had been open to receive it. June and Caroline understood what they could do in similar situations in the future.

'Ah-hah' Moments

I tell all my workshop participants not to look for answers. Answers are things we use to solidify our own positions. Look for insights. Insights mean we're learning something. Insights mean we're filling that hole in our minds called 'what we don't know we don't know'.

In all the conflicts I describe in this chapter, I was there to coach the participants towards resolution. But how can you switch from Blame Frame to Outcome Frame on your own? In the world we live in, and the 'fish tank' most of us work in, it's easy to fall into Blame Frame. It's easy to react to a conflict by finger pointing. Shifting to Outcome Frame requires some self-discipline. Conflicts are very private. Many conflicts take place inside people's heads. Often there is no confrontation at all. So you have to shift to Outcome Frame on your own. It also requires a certain amount of determination.

Here's what you can do to work out whether you're in Blame Frame or Outcome Frame. Think of a recent cross-gender conflict. Describe what you did. What frame of reference did you use? Blame or Outcome? And answer the following quizzes:

Did you:

- [ ] Decide the other person was wrong?

- [ ] Argue about who was right or wrong?

- [ ] Say, 'I'm not responsible for this!'

- [ ] Walk away in anger or shock?

- [ ] Gossip?

- [ ] Keep mulling it over?

- [ ] Get defensive?

- [ ] Feel victimized, wrongly accused, misunderstood or misinterpreted?

- [ ] Feel invalidated?

If you answered 'Yes' to any of these questions, you're in the Blame Frame.

Or, did you:

☐ Stand back and reflect?

☐ Decide you were committed to this relationship?

☐ Take responsibility for dealing with the conflict?

☐ Take proactive steps towards finding a solution?

☐ Try to look for a win-win solution?

If you answered 'Yes' to any of these questions, congratulations! You are in the Outcome Frame. Here are three simple steps to help you get to a win-win solution.

1. **Co-create a win-win solution** Affirm your mutual understanding; make sure you both feel heard and understood. You could start by saying, 'You may not have meant anything by this, but. . .' or, 'I need to clarify something.' This is the hardest part for both men and women: to stay with the conversation until it's complete. Aim for a clean slate. Brainstorm together for multiple win-win solutions for the future. Concentrate on steps 2 and 3, and keep your word.

2. **Frame the conversation** Identify the goal: 'I have a conflict, and I'm here to see a win-win solution.' or, 'There's something I need to resolve with you.' Establish that your immediate goal is mutual understanding.

3. **Check in** Ask for each other's help towards this understanding. Do not defend or disagree, or you will fall back into the Blame Frame. Seek to understand before being understood. Repeat the other person's position in your own words: 'I may have

made an assumption, but. . .' or, 'I may have misinterpreted, but. . .'

Women, don't forget: there's nothing that frustrates men more than feeling that they *are* the problem instead part of the solution. And men: there's nothing that frustrates women more than 'not being heard' and understood.

In the next chapter, we'll see what happens when conflicts reach their highest level: harassment charges. Believe it or not, most harassment cases start out as gender-based misunderstandings. But when there's harassment, or the appearance of harassment, our Anger or Shock is so intense that it's almost impossible to go from the Blame Frame to the Outcome Frame. Harassment makes everyone paranoid: men are afraid of being blamed, and women of being victimized. But as you're about to see, even this mess can be resolved by understanding gender difference.

CHAPTER 11

Preventing Harassment

The way we see the problem is the problem.

Albert Einstein, German physicist

There's no doubt about it. Harassment is the most heated and corrosive conflict in today's workplace. Feeling harassed, or being harassed or being accused of harassment sets off our most basic and primitive survival instincts. It's like taking a normal conflict and multiplying the stakes by about a hundred.

Just what is harassment? When most people hear the term, they think of 'blatant' sexual harassment, situations where one employee has made clear, aggressive sexual advances on another. These incidents still happen, but there's also a new norm. Another norm is subtle harassment, situations where innuendo, ambiguous remarks or inappropriate behaviour have escalated to the point of harassment allegations. That's what this chapter is about.

I've been called in to coach literally hundreds of companies struggling to deal with a harassment charge. What do I find? There's a conflict, with two people at the centre. But by the time

I arrive, the whole workplace has turned into a psychological disaster zone.

Harassment cases affect everyone in the office. They ruin good working relationships. They create a 'camp' mentality, forcing everyone to take sides. They eliminate trust. It can take years for companies to recover from them. Researchers from Women in Management Association report that 70 per cent of UK women state that they have encountered sexual harassment in the office. Nearly 50 per cent of working women in Finland, Sweden and the former Soviet Union report having been sexually harassed, and 70 per cent of Japanese women say that they have experienced sexual harassment in the workplace.

The fallout has been enormous. Many men tell me they don't even want to work with women who are, or have been, on file as having registered a complaint, for fear of ending up being charged with harassment. But women aren't the winners in this situation. Lack of trust between co-workers ruins the environment for everyone. According to the latest statistics, women in the U.S. who sue for harassment in court are awarded on average $250,000. In my experience, even the women who have won large suits feel it wasn't worth it. Their reputations have been tainted, they feel incomplete and many are forced to leave their jobs – and some even abandon their careers.

Men, on the other hand, say they are shocked by how fast women turn to the law court solution for harassment. For the most part, men who are charged report they had no intention to harass. They say they misinterpreted a situation and ended up charged with harassment before they knew what was going on. The result is a backlash in offices everywhere: men have decided to stay as far away from female colleagues as possible. It's definitely a lose-lose solution.

In fact, women's most common complaints of sexual harassment stem from men's words, how men put things or their tone of voice. The case of Roger and Linda, two colleagues at a London newspaper, is typical. Linda brought an action against Roger for sexually harassing her. One morning, Roger had told her, 'I love you in pink!' Not surprisingly, Linda took offence at the comment. 'It was clearly suggestive. And it wasn't the first time he had said something like that to me,' she reported. Later, Roger said he thought that he and Linda were friends, so 'anything went'. He even thought that joking around would show her how much he enjoyed working with her. But Linda said it wasn't so much what he said as the way he said it. Roger was baffled. 'What can I do? I didn't mean it the way she took it!'

It sounds extraordinary, but this kind of misunderstanding happens every day. The story of Linda and Roger didn't turn into a fully fledged harassment case because they both had the good sense – and good faith – to stand in each other's shoes, see where the other was coming from, and resolve it in a win-win manner. But, sadly, many misunderstandings like this escalate into harassment cases. Then, before we know it, they have ruined our working relationships and turned entire offices into battle-grounds.

Words and tones aren't the only things that spark misunderstandings that lead to 'subtle' harassment complaints. Body language also plays a big role. Albert, a bank manager, told me he once thought a female colleague, Shirley, was making advances to him while she was making a presentation because she tossed her hair. Shirley was a very friendly woman with long hair and she had developed the habit of tossing her hair back on her shoulders when it fell in her face. Luckily, Albert had the courage to speak up about his perception. Shirley was completely floored. 'My goodness. It has nothing to do with flirting,' she told him.

Luckily, Albert resolved his misinterpretation of Shirley's mannerism, which could have resulted in his making sexual advances to her. Albert's insight? 'I had better not make any assumptions about where women are coming from, and if I do, I had better check that I will not be acting on my own perceptual filter.' Shirley had an insight too. 'First, I thought it was Albert being some kind of a dinosaur, but when I reflected on it, it has happened to me before. I must be sending some kind of signal. I'll be more careful about it in the future.'

Of course, I'm not suggesting that real harassment does not happen. Neither men nor women deny that blatant harassment occurs at work – things like grabbing, blatant sexual comments and not taking 'no' for an answer. However, the problem today is that many fairly innocent misunderstandings have been thrown into the pot along with these abuses. This has created an atmosphere of panic that permeates many offices. It's an acute problem in the U.S., but it's definitely making its way to the U.K.

It doesn't have to be this way.

How Subtle Harassment Ruins the Work Environment

In my work as a gender consultant over the last 20 years, I have noticed a recent dramatic increase – especially in the last ten years – in what I call these 'subtle' harassment complaints. And I can bear witness that these cases have just as negative an impact on a company – and everyone who works in it – as cases of blatant harassment. So what's the difference? Almost all of these subtle harassment cases happen because of misunderstandings caused by gender differences. And like all the other misunderstandings I discuss in this book, they can be resolved.

In a typical harassment case, a woman accuses a man, though that is no longer a hard and fast rule. Men can be victims of this type of harassment too. There has usually been a build-up. The victim has been made to feel uncomfortable on repeated occasions. He or she talks about the problem to the people closest to them, whether it is family, friends or a spouse. They are often advised to do something about it. Often the only recourse is to report the incident directly to the human resources department. Human resources responds by opening a file and sometimes doing a 'workplace assessment'. This usually amounts to a list of 'he said' and 'she said'. And then it's downhill from there.

The following case from a technology company illustrates how a typical 'subtle' harassment charge unfolds. Christa, a manager at the company, accused Peter, a charismatic executive manager, of harassment. Christa claimed that Peter had repeatedly leered at her. The company had an open-plan office and several women had seen Peter looking at sexually suggestive websites at his desk during office hours. Christa said that when she had walked past Peter's desk one day, he had looked up at her and 'licked his lips'. Peter hadn't made explicit sexual advances, but his action had left Christa feeling humiliated and disempowered. She had had enough. She made a complaint to human resources, who did their job and opened a file on Peter.

Things never look worse than when they are on paper. The first thing Christa knew, the company was talking about dismissing Peter. Peter was in Shock, then Anger. The first thing he did was to hire a lawyer. And that's when the case started to take its toll at the company.

Many of the men sympathized with Peter's situation. They felt the punishment was too severe for the crime. 'He's a good manager and a funny bloke,' they said. 'This doesn't have anything to do with the kind of job he does.' A lot of the men agreed that it was inappropriate to look at those types of website at work, but they said that he 'may not have realized it could be offending others.'

A lot of the women sympathized with Christa. Many had had similar experiences with Peter and all the women were offended by the pornography and the lip-licking gesture. 'It's humiliating,' the women said. Everyone was focused on, and justifying, his or her own reaction. No one was thinking of how to resolve the situation.

I was called in several months after the complaint had been

made. There were 32 employees in the firm, including Peter and Christa, and they were divided into two camps, huddled together on either side of the room. The atmosphere was tense, to say the least. As with many of the companies I see, the harassment case had turned employees against each other and created a chilling effect. Everyone was looking over their shoulder. People felt caught in the middle and neither side was listening to the other.

The men and women were so enmeshed in the situation that they weren't thinking about solutions at all. The issue had turned into a trial, a debate about who was right and who was wrong. Everyone took sides. Peter's defenders said, 'What he looks at on his laptop in his spare time is his business.' Christa's defenders said Peter's behaviour was offensive and just wrong.

Peter and Christa's story is a classic case of what happens when companies react to harassment – as they always do – by channelling complaints through a legal, formal system. It's not that the policies themselves are wrong. Companies are required by law to have policies and procedures for dealing with sexual harassment and these policies do represent a certain type of progress. We have come a long way from 20 years ago, when sexual harassment was not even recognized. And certainly, blatant sexual harassment mustn't go unreported.

The problem is that companies mistake harassment policies for 'solutions to harassment'. Relying on harassment being resolved by these policies is the biggest ticking time bomb in today's offices, because everyone loses out. In cases of blatant harassment, making a formal complaint is obviously necessary. But in most of the harassment cases I see, which are caused by inappropriate behaviour, the 'formal ' solution does more harm than good. In the case of Christa and Peter, nobody learned anything and the atmosphere at the company was ruined.

The reason harassment policies are ineffective in such cases is that they don't get to the root of the issue. They freeze employees in Shock, Anger and Rejection, in the Blame Frame. Think of the situation as a disease with symptoms. Harassment is the symptom. Harassment policies only deal with the symptoms. But the disease still festers. The proof of this is what happens after cases like Peter and Christa's are reported. The staff are divided. Team spirit disappears. 'Lone ranger' types become the norm.

The negative atmosphere can last for years and create a stifling workplace. I recall one case where women were still leaving the company two years after a harassment incident because of the chill factor it had created. The case had put everyone on the defensive. The men at the firm warned new female lawyers that they wouldn't work with women any more. And the strangest thing was, many of those women admitted that they understood how the men felt.

Formal policies to deal with harassment don't do anything to prevent harassment problems from recurring. Policies rarely solve anything because they don't get to the root of the issue, and the root of the issue is gender difference.

How Men and Women See Harassment

When it comes to harassment, men and women definitely have at least one thing in common: they're looking for 'the rules'. As I have often said, 'Wouldn't it be nice if we came with instructions?' Well, we don't. And there are no rules for dealing with sexual harassment. There are only policies, and they aren't doing much to solve the plethora of subtle harassment cases that are ruining today's workplace.

Every harassment situation is different. Each one has it's own special context, and involves unique personalities and past experiences that complicate things. If I tried to define the rules, I would constantly be changing them to adapt to each case. Instead, what I will do here is teach you to conquer subtle harassment yourself. Going through a similar process to one you saw earlier in this book, I will show you how subtle harassment impacts both men and women – in other words, what each sex says are the challenges that harassment raises for them. This will provide you with the insights you need to resolve conflicts over harassment – you won't need rules. Once again, we'll start by hearing what men and women say about the issue when they are behind closed doors.

When I give workshops on sexual harassment, I start them in the same way as my regular gender workshops. I ask men and women what their different concerns around harassment are. This is an open enough question to get a good idea of what's really on people's minds. What I see is that men and women look at the question very differently. It's the first clue to a very important lesson we all have to learn in order to deal with the issue. Harassment isn't interpreted in the same way by men as it is by women.

What's on Men's Minds

- 'I don't know the rules.'

- 'I don't know how to act.'

- 'What's the code of conduct?'

- 'What harassment means seems to vary from woman to woman. It can even vary from day to day for the same woman!'

- 'Sometimes what women call harassment doesn't look like harassment to me.'

- 'Women make mountains out of molehills.'

Men feel confused about what harassment is. They wish they knew 'the rules'. They don't understand how behaviour that seems innocent to them, turns out to be harassment in women's eyes. As one man said, 'I told my colleague I really liked her new skirt and ended up accused of harassment! What harassment?'

How do men deal with this confusion? They become careful and cautious – even paranoid. They want to know how to act, and how to avoid ending up being charged with harassment. Women tend only to worry about harassment when it happens to someone they know, but men worry about it all the time. Women are tempted to dismiss men's fear, but they shouldn't. The fear of being wrongly accused is very much on their minds.

I recommend that women accept men's fear as legitimate, and try to learn something from it.

What's on Women's Minds

Women's concerns revolve around what I would call 'sexual innuendo'. Many women will say they resent things like compliments that have a sexual tone, such as being told they look fetching, or that a piece of clothing fits them well. For example, a woman told me about an incident one Monday at work when she told her colleagues she was exhausted after her weekend. Her male colleagues asked her, in a leering, heavily suggestive manner, 'So what were you *doing* all weekend anyway?' The woman was stunned and humiliated by having an innocent remark misconstrued in a sexual manner.

A lot of women's concerns about harassment centre on men's behaviour that makes them feel excluded or singled out because of their sex. Women resent sexual innuendo being added to situations where it doesn't belong. Many women report that, on business trips and in restaurants, men they are working with start overtly flirting with strange women and waitresses.

Men don't see why a woman would take this personally. Their behaviour is often directed at other men – to show they are one of the boys. But women find this behaviour disconcerting, even humiliating. They wonder, 'Does he respect me? Why would he act this way if he did?' Then women start to wonder about that particular man's 'character' and think 'Maybe he isn't who I thought he was.' Women who work in boardroom situations also complain about men engaging in 'locker-room talk'. Again, most men probably can't imagine what the problem is.

Many women report hearing men even talk about different women's body parts. For women, this translates as objectification – and it doesn't matter which woman men are actually talking about. This kind of communication seems to come naturally to men when they are in a group, but from a woman's perspective, it seems totally uncalled for. Other things on women's list of challenges include hearing men:

- Joke about attractive women.

- Joke about unattractive women.

- Labelling women or denigrating them.

- Telling jokes centred around sexual language.

Men are perplexed when they hear how women feel about these issues. 'Is this really harassment?' they ask. A lot of men sincerely, genuinely, don't understand what all the fuss is about. They see their colleagues acting like idiots or saying something stupid and say to themselves, 'It was just that once, it didn't mean anything.' Men come to me puzzled about complaints made against them for things like making a remark about women at a company dinner or joking with the blokes about sex. This is all they see it as – joking or an offhand remark. But like women who dismiss men's concerns about being wrongly accused, men have to accept these feelings as women's legitimate concerns – and learn from them.

It's All About How It's Interpreted

You can see that harassment doesn't impact the same way for men as for women. Men and women see different worlds and hear different stories. Women perceive men as over-protecting and excluding them, and they jump to conclusions about what men really mean when they are cautious. Men assume women lack confidence when women are trying to be inclusive, or when women take things personally. In all of these situations, reactions from one sex provoke reactions from the other and drag everyone into a downwards spiral of misunderstandings.

The key to breaking out of this downwards spiral lies in understanding perceptual filters. Filters are what lead us to misinterpret remarks and behaviour. We map the behaviour of the other sex onto our own frame of reference. Then we draw mistaken conclusions about the meaning of that behaviour, and we react in ways that provoke further misunderstandings.

This basic dynamic is the root cause of most of the sexual harassment cases I see – I would say about 90 per cent of them. Many of the very same filters we saw in Chapter 7 are at the root of harassment cases. As we saw in that chapter, nothing gets resolved if you wonder who's right and who's wrong. Understanding how the other person sees things differently is the only way to resolve subtler types of harassment.

A case at an export company shows how two people, in good faith, can end up embroiled in a harassment case because of their filters. Carla, a clerical worker, filed a harassment complaint against her boss, Edward. She claimed he had put his hands on her waist and patted her on the arm. She called human resources to get some advice on how to handle the situation. Human resources opened a file and before long Edward was formally accused of sexual harassment.

When he heard about the complaint, Edward was shocked. 'That's just the way I am. I'm a touchy-feely guy,' he said. But it was too late. As Carla explained to me, she interpreted Edward's behaviour as inappropriate and intrusive. Edward could see that for some people his behaviour might be inappropriate. But he said he and Carla had a close working relationship, and he was sure she wouldn't misconstrue his actions. For Edward, physical contact was a way to connect with clients and associates, and to strengthen bonds between them. It never occurred to him that Carla would interpret it in any other way.

When Carla understood Edward's real intentions, she was relieved. She still felt his behaviour was inappropriate, but much of the offensiveness disappeared when she realized it didn't mean what she had thought it meant. His intentions were good. Understanding that the problem was caused by filters – and not by deliberate bad intentions – made it possible for both Carla and Edward to get aligned on finding a solution. Both wanted to restore the relationship. Edward recognized that his behaviour was disempowering to Carla, so he adjusted it.

Dealing with behaviour can be simple once we've tackled the underlying assumptions, interpretations and misinterpretations that often surround harassment issues.

One reason women can interpret behaviour as a sign of harassment is that they relate a particular incident to a man's entire personality. Men call this generalizing but women don't do it in bad faith. It's just the way they tend to approach things. That's why a single sexual comment made among mixed company can have such a devastating effect on a woman. It makes her wonder if she really knows the man she thought she knew.

Men don't understand that when a group of men make comments that strike women as sexist, women will question their friendship with those men.

Since men don't understand women's way of generalizing,

men look at women's behaviour through their own filters. They think women overreact. This feeds the impression that women are out to get them and adds to their fear of being unjustly accused. They listen to what a woman is saying through their men's filter and conclude that she has a chip on her shoulder. Naturally, when men have this filter, they aren't really listening to what the woman is saying.

It's not just men that misunderstand women. Women's perceptual filters also prevent them from hearing what men are saying. If a woman doesn't understand that men *don't* draw conclusions about a person's personality from particular incidents, she will conclude that a man is in denial, or dismissing her. When men say, for example, 'He was just being one of the boys,' women take on the filter, 'He's in denial.' And that just makes women angrier. But men are just being men.

Carla and Edward's story showed how important it is for men and women to learn to stand in each other's shoes. To deal with harassment, we have to look for 'What we don't know we don't know'. And the only way to do that is to understand the filters that are shaping our perception.

Having Nothing to Forgive

As I often repeat, 'Understanding means there's nothing to forgive.' In other words, if you gain understanding first, you will never have to take the harassment-file route. The key is that when you recognize there might be a misunderstanding, then follow these three basic rules:

1. Take responsibility for it as quickly as you can.

2. Don't play politics. Talking to others about what happened will only create camps. It won't help solve the problems.

3. Don't let yourself fall into the who's right and who's wrong

dynamic. It automatically puts people on the defensive. The whole office takes sides and everyone loses sight of possible solutions.

Four Guidelines for Stopping Harassment

Many offices have tried to solve harassment with a one-size-fits-all, zero-tolerance policy. Those policies never work, and for one simple reason: they are still in the Blame Frame. The key to stopping harassment is to act as quickly as possible and put an end to misunderstandings before they become insurmountable.

Men and women come into my workshops hoping for a set of rules to deal with harassment. I can't give you rules, but I can give you guidelines to help you make sure you understand what happened before it's too late. If you bear these things in mind every day at work, you will be able to deal with harassment incidents before they become 'cases' in your human resources department and before they ruin the office environment. Most of all, you will be able to transform no-win situations into win-win situations.

1. **Wait until acceptance** Remember S.A.R.A. from the last chapter? It's never a good idea to try to work through an incident when you're feeling Shock (or Surprise), Anger or Resentment. This doesn't mean you have to come to terms with an incident before you try to talk to a colleague about it. You should be in the Acceptance stage. Acceptance doesn't mean giving in. But you should be in a state where you can put aside your own need to 'be right', in order to gain some perspective on it. You can't put yourself in someone else's shoes to try to understand an incident until you've accepted what's happened.

   It's best to do this as soon as possible, before you've told others about the incident. When you try and get support from others before taking action, their sympathy puts them in a righteous frame of mind. The other person involved in the incident will sense this straightaway and be put on the defensive.

2. **Decide to take action** If everyone in your office is committed to a harassment-free environment, then everyone should be ready to take action as soon as they see a problem coming. The first person who recognizes a problem is usually the person who was hit hardest by the incident. In cases of harassment this is usually, but not always, the woman. But you have to take responsibility for resolving the problem even if you are the victim. The key is staying away from the Blame Frame.

3. **Talk directly to the other party** This is usually the other person involved. If there was a witness to an incident, that person can be included, but it's usually best to deal with a problem on a one-to-one basis. It's the best way to avoid a 'trial' atmosphere setting in. This rule is especially hard for women, who tend to want to gain support from co-workers when they've experienced harassing behaviour from a male colleague.

4. **Check and frame** Of course, once you've got through these three stages, it's time to talk. Use the checking and framing techniques I've described in other chapters. You might say, 'This situation happened. You may not have meant anything by it, but this is how it came across to me. I need to clarify it with you.'

Men are especially grateful when women use these techniques for addressing situations where they felt harassed. As we have seen throughout this book, men find it disempowering when a woman tells a lot of other women about an incident or problem she had with them. A man will find it refreshing when a woman comes to talk to him about what happened. Why? Because:

1. She has presented it in a non-blaming way.

2. She hasn't talked to others before giving him a chance to explain himself.

3. She hasn't confronted him in front of others, which he would have found humiliating.

I don't want to end this book with you thinking that harassment is the last word on gender difference. But in a way, we have come full circle. We've seen that men and women think and communicate differently, that they hear different words, see different worlds and speak different languages. Subtle harassment cases start when men and women misinterpret those differences and jump to the worst conclusions about what a member of the other sex means, and when men and women fail to imagine how their behaviour is construed by the other sex.

Harassment is the worst-case scenario of gender-based misunderstandings. But it doesn't have to be that way. Everything you've learned in this book about how men and women are different should help you to prevent misunderstandings from turning into harassment charges. And that goes for both men and women. Now that you know men and women have different blind spots and perceptual filters, you can use some of the simple techniques I've described to avoid misinterpretations and misunderstandings. You can 'check' to make sure you understand what the other person means, and you can 'frame' your words to make sure *your* real intentions come across.

I started this book as a conversation about gender difference. Now I encourage you to carry on that conversation. Take any chapter of this book and use it to start a discussion among your co-workers. Whether it's to talk about the challenges of working with the opposite sex, or about how you interpret words and actions differently, every chapter in this book can be used to start investigating gender difference in a non-blaming way. Every topic discussed can be used to help you and your co-workers to move from a denying to a tolerant attitude towards differences, and to see how gender differences can be beneficial to everyone.

It seems a strange thing to say at the end of a book on 'differences', but men and women have more in common than they think. We all want to bring pride and joy back to the workplace. Understanding gender difference is the key to unlocking that dream.

Afterword

One of the most crucial steps in business today, is the system seeing itself.

Peter Senge, author, Fifth Discipline

I started this book with the story of a law firm which had such a corrosive environment that the employees were literally 'dying' from working there. This whole book, in fact, has been a long conversation about what was going on at the law firm. It has been a conversation about gender, about how men and women are different, and how understanding those differences is the key to creating a workplace where everyone feels valued and where men and women both thrive.

Throughout this book we have looked at the workplace through the eyes of gender, but the conversation could actually have been about something else. It could have been about diversity, or inclusiveness or respect, or any one of the huge issues being debated in today's businesses. But no matter what issue you're talking about, and no matter what issue you're addressing – whether it's building 'inclusive leadership', retaining talent, or constructing an empowering culture – the fact is, there are two genders. Whatever way you try to improve your business, you're bound to encounter gender. You've seen why. Men and women look at most things through different eyes. Even when they hear the same words, they speak different languages.

And perhaps gender is just the first 'conversation' of many. For hundreds of years we've been building a workplace that suits red fish – men. The aquarium was filled with water that suited those fish. The blue fish have arrived and the water doesn't suit them nearly as well. And we've seen that when the blue fish are frustrated, the red fish really feel it. But women aren't the only kind of new fish in the old tank. The global economy means more varieties of fish are being added to the water than ever. And the blue fish are also going to work in other types of fish tank. So we had better get used to examining the water. And if we want all the fish to thrive, we have to be ready to change it.

Companies often call me in to solve a specific problem. They call it Gender, Diversity, Work-life Harmony, Conflicts, Harassment, Retention. But it really doesn't matter what they identify as the challenge to solve. It's having 'gender conversation' that counts. And the companies that have that conversation show these results:

- Their staff turnover decreases.

- Their reputations improve as great places to work in.

- Their abilites to attract talented workers increase dramatically.

- Their productivity increases.

- Their employees feel happier at work.

And what do the individuals who work at those companies get out of the conversation? Some come out of it saying, 'I can really make a difference in the way things work around here.' Some realize that leaving, or 'leaving and staying', is not the only option.

Almost all of them say they found tremendous value in talking about gender, and now feel that they're part of a worthwhile project: building a new business environment in which everyone is valued and everyone thrives. It's about capitalizing on our different strengths.

I invite you to apply the lessons and tools you've learned in this book. When you do, you'll discover that:

- You will work more effectively with the opposite sex.

- Your level of stress at work will decrease.

- You will finally feel valued and understood.

- Your job will be more fun – you will want to go to work!

The premise of this book is that men and women are different, and it's a good thing they are. The bottom line is that *all* people are different, and that's also a good thing. We can no longer afford to blame each other for our differences. We all know too well what a lose-lose world that creates.

I have often said, 'Wouldn't it be amazing if somehow men could speak for women, and women could speak for men?' Imagine the spirit of collaboration that would exist at work – and everywhere else – if that happened. Maybe that's what it would take for business leaders to realize that the gender problem is not about 'getting the numbers right'. It's about men and women being able to see the world through each other's eyes. That's what I would call a true spirit of inclusiveness.

On your way to the office tomorrow, try to imagine how that new spirit would feel. And then get the conversation rolling.

Notes

Chapter 1

1 Gallup Study, 1.7 million workers in 101 companies in 63 different countries. www.strengthfinder.org

Chapter 3

1 S.F. Witelson, I.I. Glezer and D.L. Kigar, 'Women have greater density of neurons in posterior temporal cortex', *Journal of Neuroscience* 15, 1995.
2 Dr Roger Gorski, a professor of Anatomy and Cell Biology at the University of California in Los Angeles.
3 Dr Ruben Gur, neuroscientist, University of Pennsylvania.
4 S.F. Witelson, neuroscientist, McMaster University, *Journal of Neuroscience*.
5 Deloitte & Touche, in collaboration with the Fortune Marketing Research Group, polled hundreds of businessmen and businesswomen about the skills they thought women needed to acquire to be more effective in business.
6 Dr Helen Fisher, anthropologist, author of *The First Sex*.
7 Dr Ruben Gur, neuroscientist, University of Pennsylvania.
8 Dr Laura Cousino Klein, UCLA Study – Gender & Stress, University of California, Los Angeles, 2001.
9 Yerkes Regional Primate Research Center, Emory University, Atlanta, Georgia.

Chapter 8

1 Du Pont Study – Work/Life Balance & Quality of Life.

Chapter 10

1 Walter Ong, linguist, author of *Fighting for Life*, discussing men's reaction to conflict.
2 Howard Bloom, paleopsychologist, author of *The Global Brain*, writes that 'in organizations, men spend more time 'posturing', and in hierarchical displays' or 'territorial competitions'.
3 Deborah Tannen, linguist, in her recent book, *The Argument Culture*.
4 John Gottman and Robert Levenson, psychologists at the University of Washington, 'you can see the differences in how men and women react to conflict by simply observing the physiological changes conflict provokes.'
5 Virginia Satir, family therapist and author of *People Making*, Science and Behaviour Books, Inc., Palo Alto, California.

Further Reading

Amen, D.G., *Change Your Brain, Change Your Life*, IBS Books, 1999.

Andreae, S., *Anatomy of Desire: The Science and Psychology of Sex, Love and Marriage*, Little, Brown, 1998.

Arburdene, P. & Naisbitt, J., *Megatrends for Women, From Liberation to Leadership*, Arrow, 1994.

Archer, J. & Lloyd, B., *Sex and Gender*, Cambridge University Press, 1995.

Bloom, H., *Global Brain: The Evolution of Mass Mind from the Big Bang to the 21st Century*, John Wiley & Sons, 2001.

Blum, D., *Sex on the Brain*, Penguin, 1998.

Burr, C.I., *A Separate Creation*, Bantam Press, 1997.

Canary, D.J. & Emmers-Sommer, T.M., *Sex and Gender Differences in Personal Relationships*, Guildford Press, 1998.

Carper, J., *Your Miracle Brain*, HarperCollins, 2001.

Coates, J., *Women, Men and Language*, Longman, 1993.

Covey, S., *The 7 Habits of Highly Effective People: Powerful Lessons in Personal Change,* Simon & Schuster, 2002.

Fisher, H., *The First Sex: The Natural Talents of Women and How They Are Changing the World*, Ballantine Books, 1999.

Gardner, H., *Extraordinary Minds*, Phoenix, 1998.

Gilligan, C., *In a Different Voice*, Harvard University Press, 1982.

Gray, J., *Men, Women and Relationships*, Beyond Words, 1993.

Helgesen, S., *The Female Advantage: Women's Way of Leadership*, Doubleday, 1995.

Hendrix, H., *Getting the Love You Want: A Guide for Couples*, Pocket Books, 1993.

Humphrey, N., *A History of the Mind*, Vintage, 1993.

Jensen, E., *Brain-based Learning*, Turning Point Publications, 1995.

Maccoby, E., *The Psychology of Sex Differences*, Stanford University Press, 1974.

Markova, D., *Open Mind*, Conari Press, 1997.

Moir, A. & Jessel, D., *Brain Sex*, Mandarin, 1991.

Ong, W.J., *Fighting for Life Contest, Sexuality and Consciousness*, Cornell University Press, 1981.

Reisner, P., *Couplehood*, Bantam Press, 1994.

Saint Onge, H., *Leveraging Communities of Practice*, Butterworth-Heinemann, 2002.

Stone, D., Patton, B. & Heen, S., *Difficult Conversations, How to Discuss What Matters Most*, Penguin, 1999.

Tannen, D., *That's Not What I Meant*, Virago Press, 1992.

Tannen, D, *You Just Don't Understand: Women and Men in Conversation*, Virago Press, 1990.

Tannen, D, *The Argumentative Culture: Stopping America's War of Words*, Virago Press, 1999.

Index

About Barbara Annis

Barbara Annis is the Chief Executive Officer of Barbara Annis & Associates Inc. Her firm is the recognized leading expert in Gender, Diversity and Cultural Inclusiveness in North America and Europe. It is dedicated to removing organizational barriers by bringing the latest research and thinking on Gender Differences & Cultural Diversity into the workplace so that organizations can turn diversity into a powerful technology of success. Over the last 15 years, Barbara Annis & Associates has facilitated over 2,000 corporate workshops and information sessions on Gender & Diversity for North American and European businesses in both the public and the private sectors.

Barbara's firm is committed to creating workplace cultures that acknowledge, value and optimize the unique differences and capabilities men and women can contribute in working together towards inclusiveness and breakthrough results.

Services Available

Barbara Annis speaks to conventions and organizations all over the world. She also has senior associates who can facilitate Lunch & Learn Sessions or Public Workshops in most languages around the world. In addition, Barbara Annis & Associates Inc. conducts seminars, coaching sessions and in-depth consulting in the following: Executive Coaching, Diagnostic Tools & Strategy, Train the Trainer, Gender, Diversity, Preventing Harassment, Transformational Leadership, Attraction & Retention, Breakthrough Teams, Increased Productivity, Customer Service, and Selling & Marketing to Women.

For further information please contact:

Barbara Annis & Associates Inc.
www.BaaInc.com

Products

For stand-alone products such as training kits, tool kits, research, articles, audio tapes, video tapes or DVDs, please contact: www.gsparrow@BaaInc.com

Public Workshops

To register for public workshops or current events please contact us at: www.BaaInc.com

Notes

The notes to this book may be found on the author's website at: www.SWDL.comhttp://www.swdl.com/